Memoirs of Casanova Volume X

Memoirs of Casanova Volume X

Giacomo Casanova

MINT EDITIONS

Memoirs of Casanova Volume X was first published in 1902.

This edition published by Mint Editions 2021.

ISBN 9781513281926 | E-ISBN 9781513286945

Published by Mint Editions®

MINT EDITIONS

minteditionbooks.com

Publishing Director: Jennifer Newens
Design & Production: Rachel Lopez Metzger
Project Manager: Micaela Clark
Translated By: Arthur Machen
Typesetting: Westchester Publishing Services

Contents

I

Under the Leads—The Earthquake

W hat a strange and unexplained power certain words exercise upon the soul! I, who the evening before so bravely fortified myself with my innocence and courage, by the word tribunal was turned to a stone, with merely the faculty of passive obedience left to me.

My desk was open, and all my papers were on a table where I was accustomed to write.

"Take them," said I, to the agent of the dreadful Tribunal, pointing to the papers which covered the table. He filled a bag with them, and gave it to one of the sbirri, and then told me that I must also give up the bound manuscripts which I had in my possession. I shewed him where they were, and this incident opened my eyes. I saw now, clearly enough, that I had been betrayed by the wretch Manuzzi. The books were, "The Key of Solomon the King," "The Zecorben," a "Picatrix," a book of "Instructions on the Planetary Hours," and the necessary incantations for conversing with demons of all sorts. Those who were aware that I possessed these books took me for an expert magician, and I was not sorry to have such a reputation.

Messer-Grande took also the books on the table by my bed, such as Petrarch, Ariosto, Horace. "The Military' Philosopher" (a manuscript which Mathilde had given me), "The Porter of Chartreux," and "The Aretin," which Manuzzi had also denounced, for Messer-Grande asked me for it by name. This spy, Manuzzi, had all the appearance of an honest man—a very necessary qualification for his profession. His son made his fortune in Poland by marrying a lady named Opeska, whom, as they say, he killed, though I have never had any positive proof on the matter, and am willing to stretch Christian charity to the extent of believing he was innocent, although he was quite capable of such a crime.

While Messer-Grande was thus rummaging among my manuscripts, books and letters, I was dressing myself in an absent-minded manner, neither hurrying myself nor the reverse. I made my toilette, shaved myself, and combed my hair; putting on mechanically a laced shirt and my holiday suit without saying a word, and without Messer-Grande—who did not let me escape his sight for an instant—complaining that I was dressing myself as if I were going to a wedding.

As I went out I was surprised to see a band of forty men-at-arms in the ante-room. They had done me the honour of thinking all these men necessary for my arrest, though, according to the axiom 'Ne Hercules quidem contra duos', two would have been enough. It is curious that in London, where everyone is brave, only one man is needed to arrest another, whereas in my dear native land, where cowardice prevails, thirty are required. The reason is, perhaps, that the coward on the offensive is more afraid than the coward on the defensive, and thus a man usually cowardly is transformed for the moment into a man of courage. It is certain that at Venice one often sees a man defending himself against twenty sbirri, and finally escaping after beating them soundly. I remember once helping a friend of mine at Paris to escape from the hands of forty bum-bailiffs, and we put the whole vile rout of them to flight.

Messer-Grande made me get into a gondola, and sat down near me with an escort of four men. When we came to our destination he offered me coffee, which I refused; and he then shut me up in a room. I passed these four hours in sleep, waking up every quarter of an hour to pass water—an extraordinary occurrence, as I was not at all subject to stranguary; the heat was great, and I had not supped the evening before. I have noticed at other times that surprise at a deed of oppression acts on me as a powerful narcotic, but I found out at the time I speak of that great surprise is also a diuretic. I make this discovery over to the doctors, it is possible that some learned man may make use of it to solace the ills of humanity. I remember laughing very heartily at Prague six years ago, on learning that some thin-skinned ladies, on reading my flight from The Leads, which was published at that date, took great offence at the above account, which they thought I should have done well to leave out. I should have left it out, perhaps, in speaking to a lady, but the public is not a pretty woman whom I am intent on cajoling, my only aim is to be instructive. Indeed, I see no impropriety in the circumstance I have narrated, which is as common to men and women as eating and drinking; and if there is anything in it to shock too sensitive nerves, it is that we resemble in this respect the cows and pigs.

It is probable that just as my overwhelmed soul gave signs of its failing strength by the loss of the thinking faculty, so my body distilled a great part of those fluids which by their continual circulation set the thinking faculty in motion. Thus a sudden shock might cause instantaneous death, and send one to Paradise by a cut much too short.

In course of time the captain of the men-at-arms came to tell me that he was under orders to take me under the Leads. Without a word I followed him. We went by gondola, and after a thousand turnings among the small canals we got into the Grand Canal, and landed at the prison quay. After climbing several flights of stairs we crossed a closed bridge which forms the communication between the prisons and the Doge's palace, crossing the canal called Rio di Palazzo. On the other side of this bridge there is a gallery which we traversed. We then crossed one room, and entered another, where sat an individual in the dress of a noble, who, after looking fixedly at me, said, "E quello, mettetelo in deposito:"

This man was the secretary of the Inquisitors, the prudent Dominic Cavalli, who was apparently ashamed to speak Venetian in my presence as he pronounced my doom in the Tuscan language.

Messer-Grande then made me over to the warden of The Leads, who stood by with an enormous bunch of keys, and accompanied by two guards, made me climb two short flights of stairs, at the top of which followed a passage and then another gallery, at the end of which he opened a door, and I found myself in a dirty garret, thirty-six feet long by twelve broad, badly lighted by a window high up in the roof. I thought this garret was my prison, but I was mistaken; for, taking an enormous key, the gaoler opened a thick door lined with iron, three and a half feet high, with a round hole in the middle, eight inches in diameter, just as I was looking intently at an iron machine. This machine was like a horse shoe, an inch thick and about five inches across from one end to the other. I was thinking what could be the use to which this horrible instrument was put, when the gaoler said, with a smile,

"I see, sir, that you wish to know what that is for, and as it happens I can satisfy your curiosity. When their excellencies give orders that anyone is to be strangled, he is made to sit down on a stool, the back turned to this collar, and his head is so placed that the collar goes round one half of the neck. A silk band, which goes round the other half, passes through this hole, and the two ends are connected with the axle of a wheel which is turned by someone until the prisoner gives up the ghost, for the confessor, God be thanked! never leaves him till he is dead."

"All this sounds very ingenious, and I should think that it is you who have the honour of turning the wheel."

He made no answer, and signing to me to enter, which I did by bending double, he shut me up, and afterwards asked me through the grated hole what I would like to eat.

"I haven't thought anything about it yet," I answered. And he went away, locking all the doors carefully behind him.

Stunned with grief, I leant my elbows on the top of the grating. It was crossed, by six iron bars an inch thick, which formed sixteen square holes. This opening would have lighted my cell, if a square beam supporting the roof which joined the wall below the window had not intercepted what little light came into that horrid garret. After making the tour of my sad abode, my head lowered, as the cell was not more than five and a half feet high, I found by groping along that it formed three-quarters of a square of twelve feet. The fourth quarter was a kind of recess, which would have held a bed; but there was neither bed, nor table, nor chair, nor any furniture whatever, except a bucket—the use of which may be guessed, and a bench fixed in the wall a foot wide and four feet from the ground. On it I placed my cloak, my fine suit, and my hat trimmed with Spanish paint and adorned with a beautiful white feather. The heat was great, and my instinct made me go mechanically to the grating, the only place where I could lean on my elbows. I could not see the window, but I saw the light in the garret, and rats of a fearful size, which walked unconcernedly about it; these horrible creatures coming close under my grating without shewing the slightest fear. At the sight of these I hastened to close up the round hole in the middle of the door with an inside shutter, for a visit from one of the rats would have frozen my blood. I passed eight hours in silence and without stirring, my arms all the time crossed on the top of the grating.

At last the clock roused me from my reverie, and I began to feel restless that no one came to give me anything to eat or to bring me a bed whereon to sleep. I thought they might at least let me have a chair and some bread and water. I had no appetite, certainly; but were my gaolers to guess as much? And never in my life had I been so thirsty. I was quite sure, however, that somebody would come before the close of the day; but when I heard eight o'clock strike I became furious, knocking at the door, stamping my feet, fretting and fuming, and accompanying this useless hubbub with loud cries. After more than an hour of this wild exercise, seeing no one, without the slightest reason to think I could be heard, and shrouded in darkness, I shut the grating for fear of the rats, and threw myself at full length upon the floor. So cruel a desertion seemed to me unnatural, and I came to the conclusion that the Inquisitors had sworn my death. My investigation as to what I had done to deserve such a fate was not a long one, for in the most scrupulous examination of my conduct I could find no crimes. I was, it is true, a profligate, a gambler, a bold talker, a man who thought of little besides enjoying this present life, but in all that there was no offence against the state. Nevertheless, finding myself treated as a criminal, rage and despair made me express myself against the horrible despotism which oppressed me in a manner which I will leave my readers to guess, but which I will not repeat here. But notwithstanding my brief and anxiety, the hunger which began to make itself felt, and the thirst which tormented me, and the hardness of the boards on which I lay, did not prevent exhausted nature from reasserting her rights; I fell asleep.

My strong constitution was in need of sleep; and in a young and healthy subject this imperious necessity silences all others, and in this way above all is sleep rightly termed the benefactor of man.

The clock striking midnight awoke me. How sad is the awaking when it makes one regret one's empty dreams. I could scarcely believe that I had spent three painless hours. As I lay on my left side, I stretched out my right hand to get my handkerchief, which I remembered putting on that side. I felt about for it, when—heavens! what was my surprise to feel another hand as cold as ice. The fright sent an electric shock through me, and my hair began to stand on end.

Never had I been so alarmed, nor should I have previously thought myself capable of experiencing such terror. I passed three or four minutes in a kind of swoon, not only motionless but incapable of thinking. As I got back my senses by degrees, I tried to make myself believe that the hand I fancied I had touched was a mere creature of my disordered imagination; and with this idea I stretched out my hand again, and again with the same result. Benumbed with fright, I uttered a piercing cry, and, dropping the hand I held, I drew back my arm, trembling all over:

Soon, as I got a little calmer and more capable of reasoning, I concluded that a corpse had been placed beside me whilst I slept, for I was certain it was not there when I lay down.

"This," said I, "is the body of some strangled wretch, and they would thus warn me of the fate which is in store for me."

The thought maddened me; and my fear giving place to rage, for the third time I stretched my arm towards the icy hand, seizing it to make certain of the fact in all its atrocity, and wishing to get up, I rose upon my left elbow, and found that I had got hold of my other hand. Deadened by the weight of my body and the hardness of the boards, it had lost warmth, motion, and all sensation.

In spite of the humorous features in this incident, it did not cheer me up, but, on the contrary, inspired me with the darkest fancies. I saw that I was in a place where, if the false appeared true, the truth might appear false, where understanding was bereaved of half its prerogatives, where the imagination becoming affected would either make the reason a victim to empty hopes or to dark despair. I resolved to be on my guard; and for the first time in my life, at the age of thirty, I called philosophy to my assistance. I had within me all the seeds of philosophy, but so far I had had no need for it.

I am convinced that most men die without ever having thought, in the proper sense of the word, not so much for want of wit or of good sense, but rather because the shock necessary to the reasoning faculty in its inception has never occurred to them to lift them out of their daily habits.

After what I had experienced, I could think of sleep no more, and to get up would have been useless as I could not stand upright, so I took the only sensible course and remained seated. I sat thus till four o'clock in the morning, the sun would rise at five, and I longed to see the day, for a presentiment which I held infallible told me that it would set me again at liberty. I was consumed with a desire for revenge, nor did I conceal it from myself. I saw myself at the head of the people, about to exterminate the Government which had oppressed me; I massacred all the aristocrats without pity; all must be shattered and brought to the dust. I was delirious; I knew the authors of my misfortune, and in my fancy I destroyed them. I restored the natural right common to all men of being obedient only to the law, and of being tried only by their peers and by laws to which they have agreed-in short, I built castles in Spain. Such is man when he has become the prey of a devouring passion. He does not suspect that the principle which moves him is not reason but wrath, its greatest enemy.

I waited for a less time than I had expected, and thus I became a little more quiet. At half-past four the deadly silence of the place—this hell of the living—was broken by the shriek of bolts being shot back in the passages leading to my cell.

"Have you had time yet to think about what you will take to eat?" said the harsh voice of my gaoler from the wicket.

One is lucky when the insolence of a wretch like this only shews itself in the guise of jesting. I answered that I should like some rice soup, a piece of boiled beef, a roast, bread, wine, and water. I saw that the lout was astonished not to hear the lamentations he expected. He went away and came back again in a quarter of an hour to say that he was astonished I did not require a bed and the necessary pieces of furniture, "for," said he, "if you flatter yourself that you are only here for a night, you are very much mistaken."

"Then bring me whatever you think necessary."

"Where shall I go for it? Here is a pencil and paper; write it down."

I skewed him by writing where to go for my shirts, stockings, and clothes of all sorts, a bed, table, chair, the books which Messer-Grande had confiscated, paper, pens, and so forth. On my reading out the list to him (the lout did not know how to read) he cried, "Scratch out," said he, "scratch out books, paper, pens, looking-glass and razors, for all that is forbidden fruit here, and then give me some money to get your dinner." I had three sequins so I gave him one, and he went off. He spent an hour in the passages engaged, as I learnt afterwards, in attending on seven other prisoners who were imprisoned in cells placed far apart from each other to prevent all communication.

About noon the gaoler reappeared followed by five guards, whose duty it was to serve the state prisoners. He opened: the cell door to bring in my dinner and the furniture I had asked for. The bed was placed in the recess; my dinner was laid out on a small table, and I had to eat with an ivory spoon he had procured out of the money I had given him; all forks, knives, and edged tools being forbidden.

"Tell me what you would like for to-morrow," said he, "for I can only come here once a day at sunrise. The Lord High Secretary has told me to inform you that he will send you some suitable books, but those you wish for are forbidden."

"Thank him for his kindness in putting me by myself."

"I will do so, but you make a mistake in jesting thus."

"I don't jest at all, for I think truly that it is much better to be alone than to mingle with the scoundrels who are doubtless here."

"What, sir! scoundrels? Not at all, not at all. They are only respectable people here, who, for reasons known to their excellencies alone, have to be sequestered from society. You have been put by yourself as an additional punishment, and you want me to thank the secretary on that account?"

"I was not aware of that."

The fool was right, and I soon found it out. I discovered that a man imprisoned by himself can have no occupations. Alone in a gloomy cell where he only sees the fellow who brings his food once a day, where he cannot walk upright, he is the most wretched of men. He would like to be in hell, if he believes in it, for the sake of the company. So strong a feeling is this that I got to desire the company of a murderer, of one stricken with the plague, or of a bear. The loneliness behind the prison bars is terrible, but it must be learnt by experience to be understood, and such an experience I would not wish even to my enemies. To a man of letters in my situation, paper and ink would take away nine-tenths of the torture, but the wretches who persecuted me did not dream of granting me such an alleviation of my misery.

After the gaoler had gone, I set my table near the grating for the sake of the light, and sat down to dinner, but I could only swallow a few spoonfuls of soup. Having fasted for nearly forty-eight hours, it was not surprising that I felt ill. I passed the day quietly enough seated on my sofa, and proposing myself to read the "suitable books" which they had been good enough to promise me. I did not shut my eyes the whole night, kept awake by the hideous noise made by the rats, and by the deafening chime of the clock of St. Mark's, which seemed to be striking in my room. This double vexation was not my chief trouble, and I daresay many of my readers will guess what I am going to speak of-namely, the myriads of fleas which held high holiday over me. These small insects drank my blood with unutterable voracity, their incessant bites gave me spasmodic convulsions and poisoned my blood.

At day-break, Lawrence (such was the gaoler's name) came to my cell and had my bed made, and the room swept and cleansed, and one of the guards gave me water wherewith to wash myself. I wanted to take a walk in the garret, but Lawrence told me that was forbidden. He gave me two thick books which I forbore to open, not being quite sure of repressing the wrath with which they might inspire me, and which the spy would have infallibly reported to his masters. After leaving me my fodder and two cut lemons he went away.

As soon as I was alone I ate my soup in a hurry, so as to take it hot, and then I drew as near as I could to the light with one of the books, and was delighted to find that I could see to read. I looked at the title, and read, "The Mystical City of Sister Mary of Jesus, of Agrada." I had never heard of it. The other book was by a Jesuit named Caravita. This fellow, a hypocrite like the rest of them, had invented a new cult of the "Adoration of the Sacred Heart of our Lord Jesus Christ." This, according to the author, was the part of our Divine Redeemer, which above all others should be adored a curious idea of a besotted ignoramus, with which I got disgusted at the first page, for to my thinking the heart is no more worthy a part than the lungs, stomach; or any other of the inwards. The "Mystical City" rather interested me.

I read in it the wild conceptions of a Spanish nun, devout to superstition, melancholy, shut in by convent walls, and swayed by the ignorance and bigotry of her confessors. All these grotesque, monstrous, and fantastic visions of hers were dignified with the name of revelations. The lover and bosom-friend of the Holy Virgin, she had received instructions from God Himself to write the life of His divine mother; the necessary information was furnished her by the Holy Ghost.

This life of Mary began, not with the day of her birth, but with her immaculate conception in the womb of Anne, her mother. This Sister Mary of Agrada was the head of a Franciscan convent founded by herself in her own house. After telling in detail all the deeds of her divine heroine whilst in her mother's womb, she informs us that at the age of three she swept and cleansed the house with the assistance of nine hundred servants, all of whom were angels whom God had placed at her disposal, under the command of Michael, who came and went between God and herself to conduct their mutual correspondence.

What strikes the judicious reader of the book is the evident belief of the more than fanatical writer that nothing is due to her invention; everything is told in good faith and with full belief. The work contains the dreams of a visionary, who, without vanity but inebriated with the idea of God, thinks to reveal only the inspirations of the Divine Spirit.

The book was published with the permission of the very holy and very horrible Inquisition. I could not recover from my astonishment! Far from its stirring up in my breast a holy and simple zeal of religion, it inclined me to treat all the mystical dogmas of the Faith as fabulous.

Such works may have dangerous results; for example, a more susceptible reader than myself, or one more inclined to believe in the marvellous, runs the risk of becoming as great a visionary as the poor nun herself.

The need of doing something made me spend a week over this masterpiece of madness, the product of a hyper-exalted brain. I took care to say nothing to the gaoler about this fine work, but I began to feel the effects of reading it. As soon as I went off to sleep I experienced the disease which Sister Mary of Agrada had communicated to my mind weakened by melancholy, want of proper nourishment and exercise, bad air, and the horrible uncertainty of my fate. The wildness of my dreams made me laugh when I recalled them in my waking moments. If I had possessed the necessary materials I would have written my visions down, and I might possibly have produced in my cell a still madder work than the one chosen with such insight by Cavalli.

This set me thinking how mistaken is the opinion which makes human intellect an absolute force; it is merely relative, and he who studies himself carefully will find only weakness. I perceived that though men rarely become mad, still such an event is well within the bounds of possibility, for our reasoning faculties are like powder, which, though it catches fire easily, will never catch fire at all without a spark. The book of the Spanish nun has all the properties necessary to make a man crack-brained; but for the poison to take effect he must be isolated, put under the Leads, and deprived of all other employments.

In November, 1767, as I was going from Pampeluna to Madrid, my coachman, Andrea Capello, stopped for us to dine in a town of Old Castille. So dismal and dreary a place did I find it that I asked its name. How I laughed when I was told that it was Agrada!

"Here, then," I said to myself, "did that saintly lunatic produce that masterpiece which but for M. Cavalli I should never have known."

An old priest, who had the highest possible opinion of me the moment I began to ask him about this truthful historian of the mother of Christ, shewed me the very place where she had written it, and assured me that the father, mother, sister, and in short all the kindred of the blessed biographer, had been great saints in their generation. He told me, and spoke truly, that the Spaniards had solicited her canonization at Rome, with that of the venerable Palafox. This "Mystical City," perhaps, gave Father Malagrida the idea of writing the life of St. Anne, written, also, at the dictation of the Holy Ghost, but the poor devil of a Jesuit had to suffer martyrdom for it—an additional reason for his canonization, if the horrible society ever comes to life again, and attains the universal power which is its secret aim.

At the end of eight or nine days I found myself moneyless. Lawrence asked me for some, but I had not got it.

"Where can I get some?"

"Nowhere."

What displeased this ignorant and gossiping fellow about me was my silence and my laconic manner of talking.

Next day he told me that the Tribunal had assigned me fifty sous per diem of which he would have to take charge, but that he would give me an account of his expenditure every month, and that he would spend the surplus on what I liked.

"Get me the Leyden Gazette twice a week."

"I can't do that, because it is not allowed by the authorities."

Sixty-five livres a month was more than I wanted, since I could not eat more than I did: the great heat and the want of proper nourishment had weakened me. It was in the dog-days; the strength of the sun's rays upon the lead of the roof made my cell like a stove, so that the streams of perspiration which rolled off my poor body as I sat quite naked on my sofa-chair wetted the floor to right and left of me.

I had been in this hell-on-earth for fifteen days without any secretion from the bowels. At the end of this almost incredible time nature re-asserted herself, and I thought my last hour was come. The haemorrhoidal veins were swollen to such an extent that the pressure on them gave me almost unbearable agony. To this fatal time I owe the inception of that sad infirmity of which I have never been able to completely cure myself. The recurrence of the same pains, though not so acute, remind me of the cause, and do not make my remembrance of it any the more agreeable. This disease got me compliments in Russia when I was there ten years later, and I found it in such esteem that I did not dare to complain. The same kind of thing happened to me at Constantinople, when I was complaining of a cold in the head in the presence of a Turk, who was thinking, I could see, that a dog of a Christian was not worthy of such a blessing.

The same day I sickened with a high fever and kept my bed. I said nothing to Lawrence about it, but the day after, on finding my dinner untouched, he asked me how I was.

"Very well."

"That can't be, sir, as you have eaten nothing. You are ill, and you will experience the generosity of the Tribunal who will provide you, without fee or charge, with a physician, surgeon, and all necessary medicines."

He went out, returning after three hours without guards, holding a candle in his hand, and followed by a grave-looking personage; this was the doctor. I was in the height of the fever, which had not left me for three days. He came up to me and began to ask me questions, but I told him that with my confessor and my doctor I would only speak apart. The doctor told Lawrence to leave the room, but on the refusal of that Argus to do so, he went away saying that I was dangerously ill, possibly unto death. For this I hoped, for my life as it had become was no longer my chiefest good. I was somewhat glad also to think that my pitiless persecutors might, on hearing of my condition, be forced to reflect on the cruelty of the treatment to which they had subjected me.

Four hours afterwards I heard the noise of bolts once more, and the doctor came in holding the candle himself. Lawrence remained outside. I had become so weak that I experienced a grateful restfulness. Kindly nature does not suffer a man seriously ill to feel weary. I was delighted to hear that my infamous turnkey was outside, for since his explanation of the iron collar I had looked an him with loathing.

In a quarter of an hour I had told the doctor all.

"If we want to get well," said he, "we must not be melancholy."

"Write me the prescription, and take it to the only apothecary who can make it up. M. Cavalli is the bad doctor who exhibited 'The Heart of Jesus,' and 'The Mystical City.'"

"Those two preparations are quite capable of having brought on the fever and the haemorrhoids. I will not forsake you."

After making me a large jug of lemonade, and telling the to drink frequently, he went away. I slept soundly, dreaming fantastic dreams.

In he morning the doctor came again with Lawrence and a surgeon, who bled me. The doctor left me some medicine which he told me to take in the evening, and a bottle of soap. "I have obtained leave," said he, "for you to move into the garret where the heat is less, and the air better than here."

"I decline the favour, as I abominate the rats, which you know nothing about, and which would certainly get into my bed."

"What a pity! I told M. Cavalli that he had almost killed you with his books, and he has commissioned me to take them back, and to give you Boethius; and here it is."

"I am much obliged to you. I like it better than Seneca, and I am sure it will do me good."

"I am leaving you a very necessary instrument, and some barley water for you to refresh yourself with."

He visited me four times, and pulled me through; my constitution did the rest, and my appetite returned. At the beginning of September

I found myself, on the whole, very well, suffering from no actual ills except the heat, the vermin, and weariness, for I could not be always reading Boethius.

One day Lawrence told me that I might go out of my cell to wash myself whilst the bed was being made and the room swept. I took advantage of the favour to walk up and down for the ten minutes taken by these operations, and as I walked hard the rats were alarmed and dared not shew themselves. On the same day Lawrence gave me an account of my money, and brought himself in as my debtor to the amount of thirty livres, which however, I could not put into my pocket. I left the money in his hands, telling him to lay it out on masses on my behalf, feeling sure that he would make quite a different use of it, and he thanked me in a tone that persuaded me he would be his own priest. I gave him the money every month, and I never saw a priest's receipt. Lawrence was wise to celebrate the sacrifice at the tavern; the money was useful to someone at all events.

I lived from day to day, persuading myself every night that the next day I should be at liberty; but as I was each day deceived, I decided in my poor brain that I should be set free without fail on the 1st of October, on which day the new Inquisitors begin their term of office. According to this theory, my imprisonment would last as long as the authority of the present Inquisitors, and thus was explained the fact that I had seen nothing of the secretary, who would otherwise have undoubtedly come to interrogate, examine, and convict me of my crimes, and finally to announce my doom. All this appeared to me unanswerable, because it seemed natural, but it was fallacious under the Leads, where nothing is done after the natural order. I imagined the Inquisitors must have discovered my innocence and the wrong they had done me, and that they only kept me in prison for form's sake, and to protect their repute from the stain of committing injustice; hence I concluded that they would give me my freedom when they laid down their tyrannical authority. My mind was so composed and quiet that I felt as if I could forgive them, and forget the wrong that they had done me. "How can they leave me here to the mercy of their successors," I thought, "to whom they cannot leave any evidence capable of condemning me?" I could not believe that my sentence had been pronounced and confirmed, without my being told of it, or of the reasons by which my judges had been actuated. I was so certain that I had right on my side, that I reasoned accordingly; but this was not the attitude I should have assumed towards a court which stands aloof from all the courts in the world for its unbounded absolutism. To prove anyone guilty, it is only necessary for the Inquisitors to proceed against him; so there is no need to speak to him, and when he is condemned it would be useless to announce to the prisoner his sentence, as his consent is not required, and they prefer to leave the poor wretch the feeling of hope; and certainly, if he were told the whole process, imprisonment would not be shortened by an hour. The wise man tells no one of his business, and the business of the Tribunal of Venice is only to judge and to doom. The guilty party is not required to have any share in the matter; he is like a nail, which to be driven into a wall needs only to be struck.

To a certain extent I was acquainted with the ways of the Colossus which was crushing me under foot, but there are things on earth which one can only truly understand by experience. If amongst my readers there are any who think such laws unjust, I forgive them, as I know they have a strong likeness to injustice; but let me tell them that they are also necessary, as a tribunal like the Venetian could not subsist without them. Those who maintain these laws in full vigour are senators, chosen from amongst the fittest for that office, and with a reputation for honour and virtue.

The last day of September I passed a sleepless night, and was on thorns to see the dawn appear, so sure was I that that day would make me free. The reign of those villains who had made me a captive drew to a close; but the dawn appeared, Lawrence came as usual, and told me nothing new. For five or six days I hovered between rage and despair, and then I imagined that for some reasons which to me were unfathomable they had decided to keep me prisoner for the remainder of my days. This awful idea only made me laugh, for I knew that it was in my power to remain a slave for no long time, but only till I should take it into my own hands to break my prison. I knew that I should escape or die: 'Deliberata morte ferocior'.

In the beginning of November I seriously formed the plan of forcibly escaping from a place where I was forcibly kept. I began to rack my brains to find a way of carrying the idea into execution, and I conceived a hundred schemes, each one bolder than the other, but a new plan always made me give up the one I was on the point of accepting.

While I was immersed in this toilsome sea of thought, an event happened which brought home to me the sad state of mind I was in.

I was standing up in the garret looking towards the top, and my glance fell on the great beam, not shaking but turning on its right side, and then, by slow and interrupted movement in the opposite direction, turning again and replacing itself in its original position. As I lost my balance at the same time, I knew it was the shock of an earthquake. Lawrence and the guards, who just then came out of my room, said that they too, had felt the earth tremble. In such despair was I that this incident made me feel a joy which I kept to myself, saying nothing. Four or five seconds after the same movement occurred, and I could not refrain from saying,

"Another, O my God! but stronger."

The guards, terrified with what they thought the impious ravings of a desperate madman, fled in horror.

After they were gone, as I was pondering the matter over, I found that I looked upon the overthrow of the Doge's palace as one of the events which might lead to liberty; the mighty pile, as it fell, might throw me safe and sound, and consequently free, on St. Mark's Place, or at the worst it could only crush me beneath its ruins. Situated as I was, liberty reckons for all, and life for nothing, or rather for very little. Thus in the depths of my soul I began to grow mad.

This earthquake shock was the result of those which at the same time destroyed Lisbon.

II

VARIOUS ADVENTURES—MY COMPANIONS—
I PREPARE TO ESCAPE—CHANGE OF CELL

To make the reader understand how I managed to escape from a place like the Leads, I must explain the nature of the locality.

The Leads, used for the confinement of state prisoners, are in fact the lofts of the ducal palace, and take their name from the large plates of lead with which the roof is covered. One can only reach them through the gates of the palace, the prison buildings, or by the bridge of which I have spoken called the Bridge of Sighs. It is impossible to reach the cells without passing through the hall where the State Inquisitors hold their meetings, and their secretary has the sole charge of the key, which he only gives to the gaoler for a short time in the early morning whilst he is attending to the prisoners. This is done at day-break, because otherwise the guards as they came and went would be in the way of those who have to do with the Council of Ten, as the Council meets every day in a hall called The Bussola, which the guards have to cross every time they go to the Leads.

The prisons are under the roof on two sides of the palace; three to the west (mine being among the number) and four to the east. On the west the roof looks into the court of the palace, and on the east straight on to the canal called Rio di Palazzo. On this side the cells are well lighted, and one can stand up straight, which is not the case in the prison where I was, which was distinguished by the name of 'Trave', on account of the enormous beam which deprived me of light. The floor of my cell was directly over the ceiling of the Inquisitors' hall, where they commonly met only at night after the sitting of the Council of Ten of which the whole three are members.

As I knew my ground and the habits of the Inquisitors perfectly well, the only way to escape—the only way at least which I deemed likely to succeed—was to make a hole in the floor of my cell; but to do this tools must be obtained—a difficult task in a place where all communication with the outside world was forbidden, where neither letters nor visits were allowed. To bribe a guard a good deal of money would be necessary, and I had none. And supposing that the gaoler and his two guards allowed themselves to be strangled—for my hands were my only weapons—there was always a third guard on duty at the door of the passage, which he locked and would not open till his fellow who wished to pass through gave him the password. In spite of all these difficulties my only thought was how to escape, and as Boethius gave me no hints on this point I read him no more, and as I was certain that the difficulty was only to be solved by stress of thinking I centered all my thoughts on this one object.

It has always been my opinion that when a man sets himself determinedly to do something, and thinks of nought but his design, he must succeed despite all difficulties in his path: such an one may make himself Pope or Grand Vizier, he may overturn an ancient line of kings—provided that he knows how to seize on his opportunity, and be a man of wit and pertinacity. To succeed one must count on being fortunate and despise all ill success, but it is a most difficult operation.

Towards the middle of November, Lawrence told me that Messer-Grande had a prisoner in his hands whom the new secretary, Businello, had ordered to be placed in the worst cell, and who consequently was going to share mine. He told me that on the secretary's reminding him that I looked upon it as a favour to be left alone, he answered that I had grown wiser in the four months of my imprisonment. I was not sorry to hear the news or that there was a new secretary. This M. Pierre Businello was a worthy man whom I knew at Paris. He afterwards went to London as ambassador of the Republic.

In the afternoon I heard the noise of the bolts, and presently Lawrence and two guards entered leading in a young man who was weeping bitterly; and after taking off his handcuffs they shut him up with me, and went out without saying a word. I was lying on my bed, and he could not see me. I was amused at his astonishment. Being, fortunately for himself, seven or eight inches shorter than I, he was able to stand upright, and he began to inspect my arm-chair, which he doubtless thought was meant for his own use. Glancing at the ledge above the grating he saw Boethius, took it up, opened it, and put it down with a kind of passion, probably because being in Latin it was of no use to him. Continuing his inspection of the cell he went to the left, and groping about was much surprised to find clothes. He approached the recess, and stretching out his hand he touched me, and immediately begged my pardon in a respectful manner. I asked him to sit down and we were friends.

"Who are you?" said I.

"I am Maggiorin, of Vicenza. My father, who was a coachman, kept me at school till I was eleven, by which time I had learnt to read and write; I was afterwards apprenticed to a barber, where I learnt my business thoroughly. After that I became valet to the Count of X—. I had been in the service of the nobleman for two years when his daughter came from the convent. It was my duty to do her hair, and by degrees I fell in love with her, and inspired her with a reciprocal passion. After having sworn a thousand times to exist only for one another, we gave ourselves up to the task of shewing each other marks of our affection, the result of which was that the state of the young countess discovered all. An old and devoted servant was the first to find out our connection and the condition of my mistress, and she told her that she felt in duty bound to tell her father, but my sweetheart succeeded in making her promise to be silent, saying that in the course of the week she herself would tell him through her confessor. She informed me of all this, and instead of going to confession we prepared for flight. She had laid hands on a good sum of money and some diamonds which had belonged to her mother, and we were to set out for Milan to-night. But to-day the count called me after dinner, and giving me a letter, he told me to start at once and to deliver it with my own hand to the person to whom it was addressed at Venice. He spoke to me so kindly and quietly that I had not the slightest suspicion of the fate in store for me. I went to get my cloak, said good-bye to my little wife, telling her that I should soon return. Seeing deeper below the surface than I, and perchance having a presentiment of my misfortune, she was sick at heart. I came here in hot haste, and took care to deliver the fatal letter. They made me wait for an answer, and in the mean time I went to an inn; but as I came out I was arrested and put in the guard-room, where I was kept till they brought me here. I suppose, sir, I might consider the young countess as my wife?"

"You make a mistake."

"But nature—"

"Nature, when a man listens to her and nothing else, takes him from one folly to another, till she puts him under the Leads."

"I am under the Leads, then, am I?"

"As I am."

The poor young man shed some bitter tears. He was a well-made lad, open, honest, and amorous beyond words. I secretly pardoned the countess, and condemned the count for exposing his daughter to such temptation. A shepherd who shuts up the wolf in the fold should not complain if his flock be devoured. In all his tears and lamentations he thought not of himself but always of his sweetheart. He thought that the gaoler would return and bring him some food and a bed; but I undeceived him, and offered him a share of what I had. His heart, however, was too full for him to eat. In the evening I gave him my mattress, on which he passed the night, for though he looked neat and clean enough I did not care to have him to sleep with me, dreading the results of a lover's dreams. He neither understood how wrongly he had acted, nor how the count was constrained to punish him publicly as a cloak to the honour of his daughter and his house. The next day he was given a mattress and a dinner to the value of fifteen sous, which the Tribunal had assigned to him, either as a favour or a charity, for the word justice would not be appropriate in speaking of this terrible body. I told the gaoler that my dinner would suffice for the two of us, and that he could employ the young man's allowance in saying masses in his usual manner. He agreed willingly, and having told him that he was lucky to be in my company, he said that we could walk in the garret for half an hour. I found this walk an excellent thing for my health and my plan of escape, which, however, I could not carry out for eleven months afterwards. At the end of this resort of rats, I saw a number of old pieces of furniture thrown on the ground to the right and left of two great chests, and in front of a large pile of papers sewn up into separate volumes. I helped myself to a dozen of them for the sake of the reading, and I found them to be accounts of trials, and very diverting; for I was allowed to read these papers, which had once contained such secrets. I found some curious replies to the judges' questions respecting the seduction of maidens, gallantries carried a little too far by persons employed in girls' schools, facts relating to confessors who had abused their penitents, schoolmasters convicted of pederasty with their pupils, and guardians who had seduced their wards. Some of the papers dating two or three centuries back, in which the style and the manners illustrated gave me considerable entertainment. Among the pieces of furniture on the floor I saw a warming-pan, a kettle, a fire-shovel, a pair of tongs, some old candle-sticks, some earthenware pots, and even a syringe. From this I concluded that some prisoner of distinction had been allowed to make use of these articles. But what interested me most was a straight iron bar as thick as my thumb, and about a foot and a half long. However, I left everything as it was, as my plans had not been sufficiently ripened by time for me to appropriate any object in particular.

One day towards the end of the month my companion was taken away, and Lawrence told me that he had been condemned to the prisons known as The Fours, which are within the same walls as the ordinary prisons, but belong to the State Inquisitors. Those confined in them have the privilege of being able to call the gaoler when they like. The prisons are gloomy, but there is an oil lamp in the midst which gives the necessary light, and there is no fear of fire as everything is made of marble. I heard, a long time after, that the unfortunate Maggiorin was there for five years, and was afterwards sent to Cerigo for ten. I do not know whether he ever came from there. He had kept me good company, and this I discovered as soon as he was gone, for in a few days I became as melancholy as before. Fortunately, I was still allowed my walk in the garret, and I began to examine its contents with more minuteness. One of the chests was full of fine paper, pieces of cardboard, uncut pens, and clews of pack thread; the other was fastened down. A piece of polished black marble, an inch thick, six inches long, and three broad, attracted my attention, and I possessed myself of it without knowing what I was going to do with it, and I secreted it in my cell, covering it up with my shirts.

A week after Maggiorin had gone, Lawrence told me that in all probability I should soon get another companion. This fellow Lawrence, who at bottom was a mere gabbling fool, began to get uneasy at my never asking him any questions. This fondness for gossip was not altogether appropriate to his office, but where is one to find beings absolutely vile? There are such persons, but happily they are few and far between, and are not to be sought for in the lower orders. Thus my gaoler found himself unable to hold his tongue, and thought that the reason I asked no questions must be that I thought him incapable of answering them; and feeling hurt at this, and wishing to prove to me that I made a mistake, he began to gossip without being solicited.

"I believe you will often have visitors," said he, "as the other six cells have each two prisoners, who are not likely to be sent to the Fours." I made him no reply, but he went on, in a few seconds, "They send to the Fours all sorts of people after they have been sentenced, though they know nothing of that. The prisoners whom I have charge of under the Leads are like yourself, persons of note, and are only guilty of deeds of which the inquisitive must know nothing. If you knew, sir, what sort of people shared your fate, you would be astonished, It's true that you are called a man of parts; but you will pardon me. . . You know that all men of parts are treated well here. You take me, I see. Fifty sous a day, that's something. They give three livres to a citizen, four to a gentleman, and eight to a foreign count. I ought to know, I think, as everything goes through my hands."

He then commenced to sing his own praises, which consisted of negative clauses.

"I'm no thief, nor traitor, nor greedy, nor malicious, nor brutal, as all my predecessors were, and when I have drunk a pint over and above I am all the better for it. If my father had sent me to school I should have learnt to read and write, and I might be Messer-Grande to-day, but that's not my fault. M. Andre Diedo has a high opinion of me. My wife, who cooks for you every day, and is only twenty-four, goes to see him when she will, and he will have her come in without ceremony, even if he be in bed, and that's more than he'll do for a senator. I promise you you will be always having the new-comers in your cell, but never for any length of time, for as soon as the secretary has got what he wants to know from them, he sends them to their place—to the Fours, to some fort, or to the Levant; and if they be foreigners they are sent across the frontier, for our Government does not hold itself master of the subjects of other princes, if they be not in its service. The clemency of the Court is beyond compare; there's not another in the world that treats its prisoners so well. They say it's cruel to disallow writing and visitors; but that's foolish, for what are writing and company but waste of time? You will tell me that you have nothing to do, but we can't say as much."

Such was, almost word for word, the first harangue with which the fellow honoured me, and I must say I found it amusing. I saw that if the man had been less of a fool he would most certainly have been more of a scoundrel.

The next day brought me a new messmate, who was treated as Maggiorin had been, and I thus found it necessary to buy another ivory spoon, for as the newcomers were given nothing on the first day of their imprisonment I had to do all the honours of the cell.

My new mate made me a low bow, for my beard, now four inches long, was still more imposing than my figure. Lawrence often lent me scissors to cut my nails, but he was forbidden, under pain of very heavy punishment, to let me touch my beard. I knew not the reason of this order, but I ended by becoming used to my beard as one gets used to everything.

The new-comer was a man of about fifty, approaching my size, a little bent, thin, with a large mouth, and very bad teeth. He had small grey eyes hidden under thick eyebrows of a red colour, which made him look like an owl; and this picture was set off by a small black wig, which exhaled a disagreeable odour of oil, and by a dress of coarse grey cloth. He accepted my offer of dinner, but was reserved, and said not a word the whole day, and I was also silent, thinking he would soon recover the use of his tongue, as he did the next day.

Early in the morning he was given a bed and a bag full of linen. The gaoler asked him, as he had asked me, what he would have for dinner, and for money to pay for it.

"I have no money."

"What! a moneyed man like you have no money?"

"I haven't a sou."

"Very good; in that case I will get you some army biscuit and water, according to instructions."

He went out, and returned directly afterwards with a pound and a half of biscuit, and a pitcher, which he set before the prisoner, and then went away.

Left alone with this phantom I heard a sigh, and my pity made me break the silence.

"Don't sigh, sir, you shall share my dinner. But I think you have made a great mistake in coming here without money."

"I have some, but it does not do to let those harpies know of it:"

"And so you condemn yourself to bread and water. Truly a wise proceeding! Do you know the reason of your imprisonment?"

"Yes, sir, and I will endeavour in a few words to inform you of it."

"My name is Squaldo Nobili. My father was a countryman who had me taught reading and writing, and at his death left me his cottage and the small patch of ground belonging to it. I lived in Friuli, about a day's journey from the Marshes of Udine. As a torrent called Corno often damaged my little property, I determined to sell it and to set up in Venice, which I did ten years ago. I brought with me eight thousand livres in fair sequins, and knowing that in this happy commonwealth all men enjoyed the blessings of liberty, I believed that by utilizing my capital I might make a little income, and I began to lend money, on security. Relying on my thrift, my judgment, and my knowledge of the world, I chose this business in preference to all others. I rented a small house in the neighbourhood of the Royal Canal, and having furnished it I lived there in comfort by myself; and in the course of two years I found I had made a profit of ten thousand livres, though I had expended two thousand on household expenses as I wished to live in comfort. In this fashion I saw myself in a fair way of making a respectable fortune in time; but one, day, having lent a Jew two sequins upon some books, I found one amongst them called 'La Sagesse,' by Charron. It was then I found out how good a thing it is to be able to read, for this book, which you, sir, may not have read, contains all that a man need know—purging him of all the prejudices of his childhood. With Charron good-bye to hell and all the empty terrors of a future life; one's eyes are opened, one knows the way to bliss, one becomes wise indeed. Do you, sir, get this book, and pay no heed to those foolish persons who would tell you this treasure is not to be approached."

This curious discourse made me know my man. As to Charron, I had read the book though I did not know it had been translated into Italian. The author who was a great admirer of Montaigne thought to surpass his model, but toiled in vain. He is not much read despite the prohibition to read his works, which should have given them some popularity. He had the impudence to give his book the title of one of Solomon's treatises—a circumstance which does not say much for his modesty. My companion went on as follows:

"Set free by Charron from any scruples I still might have, and from those false ideas so hard to rid one's self of, I pushed my business in such sort, that at the end of six years I could lay my hand on ten thousand sequins. There is no need for you to be astonished at that, as in this wealthy city gambling, debauchery, and idleness set all the world awry and in continual need of money; so do the wise gather what the fool drops.

"Three years ago a certain Count Seriman came and asked me to take from him five hundred sequins, to put them in my business, and to give him half profits. All he asked for was an obligation in which I promised to return him the whole sum on demand. At the end of a year I sent him seventy-five sequins, which made fifteen per cent. on his money; he gave me a receipt for it, but was ill pleased. He was wrong, for I was in no need of money, and had not used his for business purposes. At the end of the second year, out of pure generosity, I sent him the same amount; but we came to a quarrel and he demanded the return of the five hundred sequins. 'Certainly,' I said, 'but I must deduct the hundred and fifty you have already received.' Enraged at this he served me with a writ for the payment of the whole sum. A clever lawyer undertook my defence and was able to gain me two years. Three months ago I was spoken to as to an agreement, and I refused to hear of it, but fearing violence I went to the Abbe Justiniani, the Spanish ambassador's secretary, and for a small sum he let me a house in the precincts of the Embassy, where one is safe from surprises. I was quite willing to let Count Seriman have his money, but I claimed a reduction of a hundred sequins on account of the costs of the lawsuit. A week ago the lawyers on both sides came to me. I shewed them a purse of two hundred and fifty sequins, and told them they might take it, but not a penny more. They went away without saying a word, both wearing an ill-pleased air, of which I took no notice. Three days ago the Abbe Justiniani told me that the ambassador had thought fit to give permission to the State Inquisitors to send their men at once to my house to make search therein. I thought the thing impossible under the shelter of a foreign ambassador, and instead of taking the usual precautions, I waited the approach of the men-at-arms, only putting my money in a place of safety. At daybreak Messer-Grande came to the house, and asked me for three hundred and fifty sequins, and on my telling him that I hadn't a farthing he seized me, and here I am."

I shuddered, less at having such an infamous companion than at his evidently considering me as his equal, for if he had thought of me in any other light he would certainly not have told me this long tale, doubtless in the belief that I should take his part. In all the folly about Charron with which he tormented me in the three days we were together, I found by bitter experience the truth of the Italian proverb: 'Guardati da colui che non ha letto che un libro solo'. By reading the work of the misguided priest he had become an Atheist, and of this he made his boast all the day long. In the afternoon Lawrence came to tell him to come and speak with the secretary. He dressed himself hastily, and instead of his own shoes he took mine without my seeing him. He came back in half an hour in tears, and took out of his shoes two purses containing three hundred and fifty sequins, and, the gaoler going before, he went to take them to the secretary. A few moments afterwards he returned, and taking his cloak went away. Lawrence told me that he had been set at liberty. I thought, and with good reason, that, to make him acknowledge his debt and pay it, the secretary had threatened him with the torture; and if it were only used in similar cases, I, who detest the principle of torture, would be the first to proclaim its utility.

On New Year's Day, 1733, I received my presents. Lawrence brought me a dressing-gown lined with foxskin, a coverlet of wadded silk, and a bear-skin bag for me to put my legs in, which I welcomed gladly, for the coldness was unbearable as the heat in August. Lawrence told me that I might spend to the amount of six sequins a month, that I might have what books I liked, and take in the newspaper, and that this present came from M. de Bragadin. I asked him for a pencil, and I wrote upon a scrap of paper: "I am grateful for the kindness of the Tribunal and the goodness of M. de Bragadin."

The man who would know what were my feelings at all this must have been in a similar situation to my own. In the first gush of feeling I forgave my oppressors, and was on the point of giving up the idea of escape; so easily shall you move a man that you have brought low and overwhelmed with misfortune. Lawrence told me that M. de Bragadin had come before the three Inquisitors, and that on his knees, and with tears in his eyes, he had entreated them to let him give me this mark of his affection if I were still in the land of the living; the Inquisitors were moved, and were not able to refuse his request.

I wrote down without delay the names of the books I wanted.

One fine morning, as I was walking in the garret, my eyes fell on the iron bar I have mentioned, and I saw that it might very easily be made into a defensive or offensive weapon. I took possession of it, and having hidden it under my dressing-gown I conveyed it into my cell. As soon as I was alone, I took the piece of black marble, and I found that I had to my hand an excellent whetstone; for by rubbing the bar with the stone I obtained a very good edge.

My interest roused in this work in which I was but an apprentice, and in the fashion in which I seemed likely to become possessed of an instrument totally prohibited under the Leads, impelled, perhaps, also by my vanity to make a weapon without any of the necessary tools, and incited by my very difficulties (for I worked away till dark without anything to hold my whetstone except my left hand, and without a drop of oil to soften the iron), I made up my mind to persevere in my difficult task. My saliva served me in the stead of oil, and I toiled eight days to produce eight edges terminating in a sharp point, the edges being an inch and a half in length. My bar thus sharpened formed an eight-sided dagger, and would have done justice to a first-rate cutler. No one can imagine the toil and trouble I had to bear, nor the patience required to finish this difficult task without any other tools than a loose piece of stone. I put myself, in fact, to a kind of torture unknown to the tyrants of all ages. My right arm had become so stiff that I could hardly move it; the palm of my hand was covered with a large scar, the result of the numerous blisters caused by the hardness and the length of the work. No one would guess the sufferings I underwent to bring my work to completion.

Proud of what I had done, without thinking what use I could make of my weapon, my first care was to hide it in such a manner as would defy a minute search. After thinking over a thousand plans, to all of which there was some objection, I cast my eyes on my arm-chair, and there I contrived to hide it so as to be secure from all suspicion. Thus did Providence aid me to contrive a wonderful and almost inconceivable plan of escape. I confess to a feeling of vanity, not because I eventually succeeded—for I owed something to good luck—but because I was brave enough to undertake such a scheme in spite of the difficulties which might have ruined my plans and prevented my ever attaining liberty.

After thinking for three or four days as to what I should do with the bar I had made into an edged tool, as thick as a walking-stick and twenty inches long, I determined that the best plan would be to make a hole in the floor under my bed.

I was sure that the room below my cell was no other than the one in which I had seen M. Cavalli. I knew that this room was opened every morning, and I felt persuaded that, after I had made my hole, I could easily let myself down with my sheets, which I would make into a rope and fasten to my bed. Once there, I would hide under the table of the court, and in the morning, when the door was opened, I could escape and get to a place of safety before anyone could follow me. I thought it possible that a sentry might be placed in the hall, but my short pike ought to soon rid me of him. The floor might be of double or even of triple thickness, and this thought puzzled me; for in that case how was I to prevent the guard sweeping out the room throughout the two months my work might last. If I forbade them to do so, I might rouse suspicion; all the more as, to free myself of the fleas, I had requested them to sweep out the cell every day, and in sweeping they would soon discover what I was about. I must find some way out of this difficulty.

I began by forbidding them to sweep, without giving any reason. A week after, Lawrence asked me why I did so. I told him because of the dust which might make me cough violently and give me some fatal injury.

"I will make them water the floor," said he.

"That would be worse, Lawrence, for the damp might cause a plethora."

In this manner I obtained a week's respite, but at the end of that time the lout gave orders that my cell should be swept. He had the bed carried out into the garret, and on pretence of having the sweeping done with greater care, he lighted a candle. This let me know that the rascal was suspicious of something; but I was crafty enough to take no notice of him, and so far from giving up my plea, I only thought how I could put it on good train. Next morning I pricked my finger and covered my handkerchief with the blood, and then awaited Lawrence in bed. As soon as he came I told him that I had coughed so violently as to break a blood-vessel, which had made me bring up all the blood he saw. "Get me a doctor." The doctor came, ordered me to be bled, and wrote me a prescription. I told him it was Lawrence's fault, as he had persisted in having the room swept. The doctor blamed him for doing so, and just as if I had asked him he told us of a young man who had died from the same cause, and said that there was nothing more dangerous than breathing in dust. Lawrence called all the gods to witness that he had only had the room swept for my sake, and promised it should not happen again. I laughed to myself, for the doctor could not have played his part better if I had given him the word. The guards who were there were delighted, and said they would take care only to sweep the cells of those prisoners who had angered them.

When the doctor was gone, Lawrence begged my pardon, and assured me that all the other prisoners were in good health although their cells were swept out regularly.

"But what the doctor says is worth considering," said he, "and I shall tell them all about it, for I look upon them as my children."

The blood-letting did me good, as it made me sleep, and relieved me of the spasms with which I was sometimes troubled. I had regained my appetite and was getting back my strength every day, but the time to set about my work was not yet come; it was still too cold, and I could not hold the bar for any length of time without my hand becoming stiff. My scheme required much thought. I had to exercise boldness and foresight to rid myself of troubles which chance might bring to pass or which I could foresee. The situation of a man who had to act as I had, is an unhappy one, but in risking all for all half its bitterness vanishes.

The long nights of winter distressed me, for I had to pass nineteen mortal hours in darkness; and on the cloudy days, which are common enough at Venice, the light I had was not sufficient for me to be able to read. Without any distractions I fell back on the idea of my escape, and a man who always thinks on one subject is in danger of becoming a monomaniac. A wretched kitchen-lamp would have made me happy, but how am I to get such a thing? O blessed prerogative of thought! how happy was I when I thought I had found a way to possess myself of such a treasure! To make such a lamp I required a vase, wicks, oil, a flint and steel, tinder, and matches. A porringer would do for the vase, and I had one which was used for cooking eggs in butter. Pretending that the common oil did not agree with me, I got them to buy me Lucca oil for my salad, and my cotton counterpane would furnish me with wicks. I then said I had the toothache, and asked Lawrence to get me a pumice-stone, but as he did not know what I meant I told him that a musket-flint would do as well if it were soaked in vinegar for a day, and, then being applied to the tooth the pain would be eased. Lawrence told me that the vinegar I had was excellent, and that I could soak the stone myself, and he gave me three or four flints he had in his pocket. All I had to do was to get some sulphur and tinder, and the procuring of these two articles set all my wits to work. At last fortune came to my assistance.

I had suffered from a kind of rash, which as it came off had left some red spots on my arms, and occasionally caused me some irritation. I told Lawrence to ask the doctor for a cure, and the next day he brought me a piece of paper which the secretary had seen, and on which the doctor had written, "Regulate the food for a day, and the skin will be cured by four ounces of oil of sweet almonds or an ointment of flour of sulphur, but this local application is hazardous."

"Never mind the danger," said I to Lawrence; "buy me the ointment, or rather get me the sulphur, as I have some butter by me, and I can make it up myself. Have you any matches? Give me a few."

He found some in his pockets, and he gave me them.

What a small thing brings comfort in distress! But in my place these matches were no small thing, but rather a great treasure.

I had puzzled my head for several hours as to what substitute I could find for tinder—the only thing I still lacked, and which I could not ask for under any pretense whatsoever—when I remembered that I had told the tailor to put some under the armpits of my coat to prevent the perspiration spoiling the stuff. The coat, quite new, was before me, and my heart began to beat, but supposing the tailor had not put it in! Thus I hung between hope and fear. I had only to take a step to know all; but such a step would have been decisive, and I dared not take it. At last I drew nigh, and feeling myself unworthy of such mercies I fell on my knees and fervently prayed of God that the tailor might not have forgotten the tinder. After this heartfelt prayer I took my coat, unsewed it, and found-the tinder! My joy knew no bounds. I naturally gave thanks to God, since it was with confidence in Him that I took courage and searched my coat, and I returned thanks to Him with all my heart.

I now had all the necessary materials, and I soon made myself a lamp. Let the reader imagine my joy at having in a manner made light in the midst of darkness, and it was no less sweet because against the orders of my infamous oppressors. Now there was no more night for me, and also no more salad, for though I was very fond of it the need of keeping the oil to give light caused me to make this sacrifice without it costing me many pangs. I fixed upon the first Monday in Lent to begin the difficult work of breaking through the floor, for I suspected that in the tumult of the carnival I might have some visitors, and I was in the right.

At noon, on Quinquagesima Sunday, I heard the noise of the bolts, and presently Lawrence entered, followed by a thick-set man whom I recognized as the Jew, Gabriel Schalon, known for lending money to young men.

We knew each other, so exchanged compliments. His company was by no means agreeable to me, but my opinion was not asked. He began by congratulating me on having the pleasure of his society; and by way of answer I offered him to share my dinner, but he refused, saying he would only take a little soup, and would keep his appetite for a better supper at his own house.

"When?"

"This evening. You heard when I asked for my bed he told me that we would talk about that to-morrow. That means plainly that I shall have no need of it. And do you think it likely that a man like me would be left without anything to eat?"

"That was my experience."

"Possibly, but between ourselves our cases are somewhat different; and without going any farther into that question, the Inquisitors have made a mistake in arresting me, and they will be in some trouble, I am certain, as to how to atone for doing so."

"They will possibly give you a pension. A man of your importance has to be conciliated."

"True, there's not a broker on the exchange more useful than myself, and the five sages have often profited by the advice I have given them. My detention is a curious incident, which, perchance, will be of service to you."

"Indeed. How, may I ask?"

"I will get you out of here in a month's time. I know to whom to speak and what way to do it."

"I reckon on you, then."

"You may do so."

This knave and fool together believed himself to be somebody. He volunteered to inform me as to what was being said of me in the town, but as he only related the idle tales of men as ignorant as himself, he wearied me, and to escape listening to him I took up a book. The fellow had the impudence to ask me not to read, as he was very fond of talking, but henceforth he talked only to himself. I did not dare to light my lamp before this creature, and as night drew on he decided on accepting some bread and Cyprus wine, and he was afterwards obliged to do as best he could with my mattress, which was now the common bed of all new-comers.

In the morning he had a bed and some food from his own house. I was burdened with this wretched fellow for two months, for before condemning him to the Fours the secretary had several interviews with him to bring to light his knaveries, and to oblige him to cancel a goodly number of illegal agreements. He confessed to me himself that he had bought of M. Domenico Micheli the right to moneys which could not belong to the buyer till after the father of the seller was dead. "It's true," said he, "that he agreed to give me fifty per cent., but you must consider that if he died before his father I should lose all." At last, seeing that my cursed fellow did not go, I determined to light my lamp again after having made him promise to observe secrecy. He only kept his promise while he was with me, as Lawrence knew all about it, but luckily he attached no importance to the fact.

This unwelcome guest was a true burden to me, as he not only prevented me from working for my escape but also from reading. He was troublesome, ignorant, superstitious, a braggart, cowardly, and sometimes like a madman. He would have had me cry, since fear made him weep, and he said over and over again that this imprisonment would ruin his reputation. On this count I reassured him with a sarcasm he did not understand. I told him that his reputation was too well known to suffer anything from this little misfortune, and he took that for a compliment. He would not confess to being a miser, but I made him admit that if the Inquisitors would give him a hundred sequins for every day of his imprisonment he would gladly pass the rest of his life under the Leads.

He was a Talmudist, like all modern Jews, and he tried to make me believe that he was very devout; but I once extracted a smile of approbation from him by telling him that he would forswear Moses if the Pope would make him a cardinal. As the son of a rabbi he was learned in all the ceremonies of his religion, but like most men he considered the essence of a religion to lie in its discipline and outward forms.

This Jew, who was extremely fat, passed three-quarters of his life in bed; and though he often dozed in the daytime, he was annoyed at not being able to sleep at night—all the more as he saw that I slept excellently. He once took it into his head to wake me up as I was enjoying my sleep.

"What do you want?" said I; "waking me up with a start like this."

"My dear fellow, I can't sleep a wink. Have compassion on me and let us have a little talk."

"You scoundrel! You act thus and you dare to call yourself my friend! I know your lack of sleep torments you, but if you again deprive me of the only blessing I enjoy I will arise and strangle you."

I uttered these words in a kind of transport.

"Forgive me, for mercy's sake! and be sure that I will not trouble you again."

It is possible that I should not have strangled him, but I was very much tempted to do so. A prisoner who is happy enough to sleep soundly, all the while he sleeps is no longer a captive, and feels no more the weight of his chains. He ought to look upon the wretch who awakens him as a guard who deprives him of his liberty, and makes him feel his misery once more, since, awakening, he feels all his former woes. Furthermore, the sleeping prisoner often dreams that he is free again, in like manner as the wretch dying of hunger sees himself in dreams seated at a sumptuous feast.

I congratulated myself on not having commenced my great work before he came, especially as he required that the room should be swept out. The first time he asked for it to be dote, the guards made me laugh by saying that it would kill me. However, he insisted; and I had my revenge by pretending to be ill, but from interested motives I made no further opposition.

On the Wednesday in Holy Week Lawrence told us that the secretary would make us the customary visit in the afternoon, the object being to give peace to them that would receive the sacrament at Easter, and also to know if they had anything to say against the gaoler. "So, gentlemen," said Lawrence, "if you have any complaints to make of me make them. Dress yourselves fully, as is customary." I told Lawrence to get me a confessor for the day.

I put myself into full dress, and the Jew followed my example, taking leave of me in advance, so sure was he that the secretary would set him free on hearing what he had to say. "My presentiment," said he, "is of the same kind as I have had before, and I have never been deceived."

"I congratulate you, but don't reckon without your host." He did not understand what I meant.

In course of time the secretary came, and as soon as the cell-door was opened the Jew ran out and threw himself at his feet on both knees, I heard for five minutes nothing but his tears and complaints, for the secretary said not one word. He came back, and Lawrence told me to go out. With a beard of eight months' growth, and a dress made for love-making in August, I must have presented a somewhat curious appearance. Much to my disgust I shivered with cold, and was afraid that the secretary would think I was trembling with fear. As I was obliged to bend low to come out of my hole, my bow was ready made, and drawing myself up, I looked at him calmly without affecting any unseasonable hardihood, and waited for him to speak. The secretary also kept silence, so that we stood facing each other like a pair of statues. At the end of two minutes, the secretary, seeing that I said nothing, gave me a slight bow, and went away. I re-entered my cell, and taking off my clothes in haste, got into bed to get warm again. The Jew was astonished at my not having spoken to the secretary, although my silence had cried more loudly than his cowardly complaints. A prisoner of my kind has no business to open his mouth before his judge, except to answer questions. On Maundy Thursday a Jesuit came to confess me, and on Holy Saturday a priest of St. Mark's came to administer to me the Holy Communion. My confession appearing rather too laconic to the sweet son of Ignatius he thought good to remonstrate with me before giving me his absolution.

"Do you pray to God?" he said.

"From the morning unto the evening, and from the evening unto the morning, for, placed as I am, all that I feel—my anxiety, my grief, all the wanderings of my mind—can be but a prayer in the eyes of the Divine Wisdom which alone sees my heart."

The Jesuit smiled slightly and replied by a discourse rather metaphysical than moral, which did not at all tally with my views. I should have confuted him on every point if he had not astonished me by a prophecy he made. "Since it is from us," said he, "that you learnt what you know of religion, practise it in our fashion, pray like us, and know that you will only come out of this place on the day of the saint whose name you bear." So saying he gave me absolution, and left me. This man left the strongest possible impression on my mind. I did my best, but I could not rid myself of it. I proceeded to pass in review all the saints in the calendar.

The Jesuit was the director of M. Flaminio Corner, an old senator, and then a State Inquisitor. This statesman was a famous man of letters, a great politician, highly religious, and author of several pious and ascetic works written in Latin. His reputation was spotless.

On being informed that I should be set free on the feast-day of my patron saint, and thinking that my informant ought to know for certain what he told me, I felt glad to have a patron-saint. "But which is it?" I asked myself. "It cannot be St. James of Compostella, whose name I bear, for it was on the feast-day of that saint that Messer-Grande burst open my door." I took the almanac and looking for the saints' days nearest at hand I found St. George—a saint of some note, but of whom I had never thought. I then devoted myself to St. Mark, whose feast fell on the twenty-fifth of the month, and whose protection as a Venetian I might justly claim. To him, then, I addressed my vows, but all in vain, for his feast came round and still I was in prison. Then I took myself to St. James, the brother of Christ, who comes before St. Philip, but again in the wrong. I tried St. Anthony, who, if the tale told at Padua be true, worked thirteen miracles a day. He worked none for me. Thus I passed from one to the other, and by degrees I got to hope in the protection of the saints just as one hopes for anything one desires, but does not expect to come to pass; and I finished up by hoping only in my Saint Bar, and in the strength of my arms. Nevertheless the promise of the Jesuit came to pass, since I escaped from The Leads on All Hallows Day; and it is certain that if I had a patron-saint, he must be looked for in their number since they are all honoured on that day.

A fortnight after Easter I was delivered from my troublesome Israelite, and the poor devil instead of being sent back to his home had to spend two years in The Fours, and on his gaining his freedom he went and set up in Trieste, where he ended his days.

No sooner was I again alone than I set zealously about my work. I had to make haste for fear of some new visitor, who, like the Jew, might insist on the cell being swept. I began by drawing back my bed, and after lighting my lamp I lay down on my belly, my pike in my hand, with a napkin close by in which to gather the fragments of board as I scooped them out. My task was to destroy the board by dint of driving into it the point of my tool. At first the pieces I got away were not much larger than grains of wheat, but they soon increased in size.

The board was made of deal, and was sixteen inches broad. I began to pierce it at its juncture with another board, and as there were no nails or clamps my work was simple. After six hours' toil I tied up the napkin, and put it on one side to empty it the following day behind the pile of papers in the garret. The fragments were four or five times larger in bulk than the hole from whence they came. I put back my bed in its place, and on emptying the napkin the next morning I took care so to dispose the fragments that they should not be seen.

Having broken through the first board, which I found to be two inches thick, I was stopped by a second which I judged to be as thick as the first. Tormented by the fear of new visitors I redoubled my efforts, and in three weeks I had pierced the three boards of which the floor was composed; and then I thought that all was lost, for I found I had to pierce a bed of small pieces of marble known at Venice as terrazzo marmorin. This forms the usual floor of venetian houses of all kinds, except the cottages, for even the high nobility prefer the terrazzo to the finest boarded floor. I was thunderstruck to find that my bar made no impression on this composition; but, nevertheless, I was not altogether discouraged and cast down. I remembered Hannibal, who, according to Livy, opened up a passage through the Alps by breaking the rocks with axes and other instruments, having previously softened them with vinegar. I thought that Hannibal had succeeded not by aceto, but aceta, which in the Latin of Padua might well be the same as ascia; and who can guarantee the text to be free from the blunders of the copyist? All the same, I poured into the hole a bottle of strong vinegar I had by me, and in the morning, either because of the vinegar or because I, refreshed and rested, put more strength and patience into the work, I saw that I should overcome this new difficulty; for I had not to break the pieces of marble, but only to pulverize with the end of my bar the cement which kept them together. I soon perceived that the greatest difficulty was on the surface, and in four days the whole mosaic was destroyed without the point of my pike being at all damaged.

Below the pavement I found another plank, but I had expected as much. I concluded that this would be the last; that is the first to be put down when the rooms below were being ceiled. I pierced it with some difficulty, as, the hole being ten inches deep, it had become troublesome to work the pike. A thousand times I commended myself to the mercy of God. Those Free-thinkers who say that praying is no good do not know what they are talking about; for I know by experience that, having prayed to God, I always felt myself grow stronger, which fact amply proves the usefulness of prayer, whether the renewal of strength come straight from God, or whether it comes only from the trust one has in Him.

On the 25th of June, on which day the Republic celebrates the wonderful appearance of St. Mark under the form of a winged lion in the ducal church, about three o'clock in the afternoon, as I was labouring on my belly at the hole, stark naked, covered with sweat, my lamp beside me. I heard with mortal fear the shriek of a bolt and the noise of the door of the first passage. It was a fearful moment! I blew out my lamp, and leaving my bar in the hole I threw into it the napkin with the shavings it contained, and as swift as lightning I replaced my bed as best I could, and threw myself on it just as the door of my cell opened. If Lawrence had come in two seconds sooner he would have caught me. He was about to walk over me, but crying out dolefully I stopped him, and he fell back, saying,

"Truly, sir, I pity you, for the air here is as hot as a furnace. Get up, and thank God for giving you such good company."

"Come in, my lord, come in," said he to the poor wretch who followed him. Then, without heeding my nakedness, the fellow made the noble gentleman enter, and he seeing me to be naked, sought to avoid me while I vainly tried to find my shirt.

The new-comer thought he was in hell, and cried out,

"Where am I? My God! where have I been put? What heat! What a stench! With whom am I?"

Lawrence made him go out, and asked me to put on my shirt to go into the garret for a moment. Addressing himself to the new prisoner, he said that, having to get a bed and other necessaries, he would leave us in the garret till he came back, and that, in the mean time, the cell would be freed from the bad smell, which was only oil. What a start it gave me as I heard him utter the word "oil." In my hurry I had forgotten to snuff the wick after blowing it out. As Lawrence asked me no questions about it, I concluded that he knew all, and the accursed Jew must have betrayed me. I thought myself lucky that he was not able to tell him any more.

From that time the repulsion which I had felt for Lawrence disappeared.

After putting on my shirt and dressing-gown, I went out and found my new companion engaged in writing a list of what he wanted the gaoler to get him. As soon as he saw me, he exclaimed, "Ah! it's Casanova." I, too, recognised him as the Abbe and Count Fenarolo, a man of fifty, amiable, rich, and a favourite in society. He embraced me, and when I told him that I should have expected to see anybody in that place rather than him, he could not keep back his tears, which made me weep also.

When we were alone I told him that, as soon as his bed came, I should offer him the recess, begging him at the same time not to accept it. I asked him, also, not to ask to have the cell swept, saying that I would tell him the reason another time. He promised to keep all secrecy in the matter, and said he thought himself fortunate to be placed with me. He said that as no one knew why I was imprisoned, everyone was guessing at it. Some said that I was the heresiarch of a new sect; others that Madame Memmo had persuaded the Inquisitors that I had made her sons Atheists, and others that Antony Condulmer, the State Inquisitor, had me imprisoned as a disturber of the peace, because I hissed Abbe Chiari's plays, and had formed a design to go to Padua for the express purpose of killing him.

All these accusations had a certain foundation in fact which gave them an air of truth, but in reality they were all wholly false. I cared too little for religion to trouble myself to found a new one. The sons of Madame Memmo were full of wit, and more likely to seduce than to be seduced; and Master Condulmer would have had too much on his hands if he had imprisoned all those who hissed the Abbe Chiari; and as for this abbe, once a Jesuit, I had forgiven him, as the famous Father Origo, himself formerly a Jesuit, had taught me to take my revenge by praising him everywhere, which incited the malicious to vent their satire on the abbe; and thus I was avenged without any trouble to myself.

In the evening they brought a good bed, fine linen, perfumes, an excellent supper, and choice wines. The abbe ate nothing, but I supped for two. When Lawrence had wished us good night and had shut us up till the next day, I got out my lamp, which I found to be empty, the napkin having sucked up all the oil. This made me laugh, for as the napkin might very well have caught and set the room on fire, the idea of the confusion which would have ensued excited my hilarity. I imparted the cause of my mirth to my companion, who laughed himself, and then, lighting the lamp, we spent the night in pleasant talk. The history of his imprisonment was as follows:

"Yesterday, at three o'clock in the afternoon, Madame Alessandria, Count Martinengo, and myself, got into a gondola. We went to Padua to see the opera, intending to return to Venice afterwards. In the second act my evil genius led me to the gaming-table, where I unfortunately saw Count Rosenberg, the Austrian ambassador, without his mask, and about ten paces from him was Madame Ruzzini, whose husband is going to Vienna to represent the Republic. I greeted them both, and was just going away, when the ambassador called out to me, so as to be heard by everyone, 'You are very fortunate in being able to pay your court to so sweet a lady. At present the personage I represent makes the fairest land in the world no better for me than a galley. Tell the lady, I beseech you, that the laws which now prevent me speaking to her will be without force at Venice, where I shall go next year, and then I shall declare war against her.' Madame Ruzzini, who saw that she was being spoken of, asked me what the count had said, and I told her, word for word. 'Tell him,' said she, 'that I accept his declaration of war, and that we shall see who will wage it best.' I did not think I had committed a crime in reporting her reply, which was after all a mere compliment. After the opera we set out, and got here at midnight. I was going to sleep when a messenger brought me a note ordering me to go to the Bussola at one o'clock, Signor Bussinello, Secretary of the Council of Ten, having something to say to me. Astonished at such an order—always of bad omen, and vexed at being obliged to obey, I went at the time appointed, and my lord secretary, without giving me a word, ordered me to be taken here."

Certainly no fault could be less criminal than that which Count Fenarolo had committed, but one can break certain laws in all innocence without being any the less punishable. I congratulated him on knowing what his crime had been, and told him that he would be set free in a week, and would be requested to spend six months in the Bressian. "I can't think," said he, "that they will leave me here for a week." I determined to keep him good company, and to soften the bitterness of his imprisonment, and so well did I sympathize with his position that I forgot all about my own.

The next morning at day-break, Lawrence brought coffee and a basket filled with all the requisites for a good dinner. The abbe was astonished, for he could not conceive how anyone could eat at such an early hour. They let us walk for an hour in the garret and then shut us up again, and we saw no more of them throughout the day. The fleas which tormented us made the abbe ask why I did not have the cell swept out. I could not let him think that dirt and untidiness was agreeable to me, or that my skin was any harder than his own, so I told him the whole story, and shewed him what I had done. He was vexed at having as it were forced me to make him my confidant, but he encouraged me to go on, and if possible to finish what I was about that day, as he said he would help me to descend and then would draw up the rope, not wishing to complicate his own difficulties by an escape. I shewed him the model of a contrivance by means of which I could certainly get possession of the sheets which were to be my rope; it was a short stick attached by one end to a long piece of thread. By this stick I intended to attach my rope to the bed, and as the thread hung down to the floor of the room below, as soon as I got there I should pull the thread and the rope would fall down. He tried it, and congratulated me on my invention, as this was a necessary part of my scheme, as otherwise the rope hanging down would have immediately discovered me. My noble companion was convinced that I ought to stop my work, for I might be surprised, having to do several days' work before finishing the hole which would cost Lawrence his life. Should the thought of gaining my liberty at the expense of a fellow-creature have made me desist? I should have still persisted if my escape had meant death to the whole body of Venetian guards, and even to the Inquisitors themselves. Can the love of country, all holy though it be, prevail in the heart of the man whose country is oppressing him?

My good humour did not prevent my companion having some bad quarters of an hour. He was in love with Madame Alessandria, who had been a singer, and was either the mistress or the wife of his friend Martinengo; and he should have deemed himself happy, but the happier a lover is, so much the more his unhappiness when he is snatched from the beloved object. He sighed, wept, and declared that he loved a woman in whom all the noble virtues were contained. I compassionated him, and took care not to comfort him by saying that love is a mere trifle—a cold piece of comfort given to lovers by fools, and, moreover, it is not true that love is a mere trifle.

The week I had mentioned as the probable term of his imprisonment passed quickly enough, and I lost my friend, but did not waste my time by mourning for him; he was set free, and I was content. I did not beg him to be discreet, for the least doubt on that score would have wounded his noble spirit. During the week he was with me he only ate soup and fruit, taking a little Canary wine. It was I who made good cheer in his stead and greatly to his delight. Before he left we swore eternal friendship.

The next day Lawrence gave me an account of my money, and on finding that I had a balance of four sequins I gave them to him, telling him it was a present from me to his wife. I did not tell him that it was for the rent of my lamp, but he was free to think so if he chose. Again betaking myself to my work, and toiling without cessation, on the 23rd of August I saw it finished. This delay was caused by an inevitable accident. As I was hollowing out the last plank, I put my eye to a little hole, through which I ought to have seen the hall of the Inquisitors-in fact, I did see it, but I saw also at one side of the hole a surface about eight inches thick. It was, as I had feared all the time it would be, one of the beams which kept up the ceiling. I was thus compelled to enlarge my hole on the other side, for the beam would have made it so narrow that a man of my size could never have got through. I increased the hole, therefore, by a fourth, working—between fear and hope, for it was possible that the space between two of the beams would not be large enough. After I had finished, a second little hole assured me that God had blessed my labour. I then carefully stopped up the two small holes to prevent anything falling down into the hall, and also lest a ray from my lamp should be perceived, for this would have discovered all and ruined me.

I fixed my escape for the eve of St. Augustine's Day, because I knew that the Grand Council assembled on that feast, and there would consequently be nobody near the room through which I must pass in getting away. This would have been on the twenty-seventh of the month, but a misfortune happened to me on the twenty-fifth which makes me still shudder when I think of it, notwithstanding the years which have passed since then.

Precisely at noon I heard the noise of bolts, and I thought I should die; for a violent beating of the heart made me imagine my last hour was come. I fell into my easy chair, and waited. Lawrence came into the garret and put his head at the grating, and said, "I give you joy, sir, for the good news I am bringing you." At first, not being able to think of any other news which could be good to me, I fancied I had been set at liberty, and I trembled, for I knew that the discovery of the hole I had made would have caused my pardon to be recalled.

Lawrence came in and told me to follow him.

"Wait till I put on my clothes."

"It's of no consequence, as you only have to walk from this abominable cell to another, well lighted and quite fresh, with two windows whence you can see half Venice, and you can stand upright too."—I could bear no more, I felt that I was fainting. "Give me the vinegar," said I, "and go and tell the secretary that I thank the Court for this favour, and entreat it to leave me where I am."

"You make me laugh, sir. Have you gone mad? They would take you from hell to put you in heaven, and you would refuse to stir? Come, come, the Court must be obeyed, pray rise, sir. I will give you my arm, and will have your clothes and your books brought for you." Seeing that resistance was of no avail, I got up, and was much comforted at hearing him give orders for my arm-chair to be brought, for my pike was to follow me, and with it hope. I should have much liked to have been able to take the hole—the object of so much wasted trouble and hope—with me. I may say with truth that, as I came forth from that horrible and doleful place, my spirit remained there.

Leaning on Lawrence's shoulder, while he, thinking to cheer me up, cracked his foolish jokes, I passed through two narrow passages, and going down three steps I found myself in a well-lighted hall, at the end of which, on the left-hand side, was a door leading into another passage two feet broad by about twelve long, and in the corner was my new cell. It had a barred window which was opposite to two windows, also barred, which lighted the passage, and thus one had a fine view as far as Lido. At that trying moment I did not care much for the view; but later on I found that a sweet and pleasant wind came through the window when it was opened, and tempered the insufferable heat; and this was a true blessing for the poor wretch who had to breathe the sultry prison air, especially in the hot season.

As soon as I got into my new cell Lawrence had my arm-chair brought in, and went away, saying that he would have the remainder of my effects brought to me. I sat on my arm-chair as motionless as a statue, waiting for the storm, but not fearing it. What overwhelmed me was the distressing idea that all my pains and contrivances were of no use, nevertheless I felt neither sorry nor repentant for what I had done, and I made myself abstain from thinking of what was going to happen, and thus kept myself calm.

Lifting up my soul to God I could not help thinking that this misfortune was a Divine punishment for neglecting to escape when all was ready. Nevertheless, though I could have escaped three days sooner, I thought my punishment too severe, all the more as I had put off my escape from motives of prudence, which seemed to me worthy of reward, for if I had only consulted my own impatience to be gone I should have risked everything. To controvert the reasons which made me postpone my flight to the 27th of August, a special revelation would have been requisite; and though I had read "Mary of Agrada" I was not mad enough for that.

III

The Subterranean Prisons Known as the Wells—Lawrence's
Vengeance—I Enter into a Correspondence With Another
Prisoner, Father Balbi: His Character—I Plan With Him
a Means of Escape—How I Contrived to Let Him Have My
Pike I am Given a Scoundrelly Companion: His Portrait

I was thus anxious and despairing when two of the guards brought me
my bed. They went back to fetch the rest of my belongings, and for
two hours I saw no one, although the door of my cell remained open.
This unnatural delay engendered many thoughts, but I could not fix
exactly on the reason of it. I only knew that I had everything to fear, and
this knowledge made me brace up my mind so that I should be able to
meet calmly all possible misfortunes.

Besides The Leads and The Fours the State Inquisitors also possess
certain horrible subterranean cells beneath the ducal palace, where
are sent men whom they do not wish to put to death, though they be
thought worthy of it.

These subterranean prisons are precisely like tombs, but they call
them "wells," because they always contain two feet of water, which
penetrates from the sea by the same grating by which light is given, this
grating being only a square foot in size. If the unfortunates condemned
to live in these sewers do not wish to take a bath of filthy water, they
have to remain all day seated on a trestle, which serves them both for
bed and cupboard. In the morning they are given a pitcher of water,
some thin soup, and a ration of army bread which they have to eat
immediately, or it becomes the prey of the enormous water rats who
swarm in those dreadful abodes. Usually the wretches condemned to
The Wells are imprisoned there for life, and there have been prisoners
who have attained a great age. A villain who died whilst I was under the
Leads had passed thirty-seven years in The Wells, and he was forty-four
when sentenced. Knowing that he deserved death, it is possible that he
took his imprisonment as a favour, for there are men who fear nought
save death. His name was Beguelin. A Frenchman by birth, he had
served in the Venetian army during the last war against the Turks in
1716, under the command of Field-Marshal the Count of Schulenbourg,
who made the Grand Vizier raise the siege of Corfu. This Beguelin was

the marshal's spy. He disguised himself as a Turk, and penetrated into the Mussulman quarters, but at the same time he was also in the service of the Grand Vizier, and being detected in this course he certainly had reason to be thankful for being allowed to die in The Wells. The rest of his life must have been divided between weariness and hunger, but no doubt he often said, "Dum vita superest, bene est."

I have seen at Spiegelberg, in Moravia, prisons fearful in another way. There mercy sends the prisoners under sentence of death, and not one of them ever survives a year of imprisonment. What mercy!

During the two mortal hours of suspense, full of sombre thoughts and the most melancholy ideas, I could not help fancying that I was going to be plunged in one of these horrible dens, where the wretched inhabitants feed on idle hopes or become the prey of panic fears. The Tribunal might well send him to hell who had endeavoured to escape from purgatory.

At last I heard hurried steps, and I soon saw Lawrence standing before me, transformed with rage, foaming at the mouth, and blaspheming God and His saints. He began by ordering me to give him the hatchet and the tools I had used to pierce the floor, and to tell him from which of the guards I had got the tools. Without moving, and quite calmly, I told him that I did not know what he was talking about. At this reply he gave orders that I should be searched, but rising with a determined air I shook my fist at the knaves, and having taken off my clothes I said to them, "Do your duty, but let no one touch me."

They searched my mattress, turned my bed inside out, felt the cushions of my arm-chair, and found nothing.

"You won't tell me, then, where are the instruments with which you made the hole. It's of no matter, as we shall find a way to make you speak."

"If it be true that I have made a hole at all, I shall say that you gave me the tools, and that I have returned them to you."

At this threat, which made his followers smile with glee, probably because he had been abusing them, he stamped his feet, tore his hair, and went out like one possessed. The guards returned and brought me all my properties, the whetstone and lamp excepted. After locking up my cell he shut the two windows which gave me a little air. I thus found myself confined in a narrow space without the possibility of receiving the least breath of air from any quarter. Nevertheless, my situation did not disturb me to any great extent, as I must confess I thought I had got off cheaply. In spite of his training, Lawrence had not thought of turning the armchair over; and thus, finding myself still possessor of the iron bar, I thanked Providence, and thought myself still at liberty to regard the bar as means by which, sooner or later, I should make my escape.

I passed a sleepless night, as much from the heat as the change in my prospects. At day-break Lawrence came and brought some insufferable wine, and some water I should not have cared to drink. All the rest was of a piece; dry salad, putrid meat, and bread harder than English biscuit. He cleaned nothing, and when I asked him to open the windows he seemed not to hear me; but a guard armed with an iron bar began to sound all over my room, against the wall, on the floor, and above all under my bed. I looked on with an unmoved expression, but it did not escape my notice that the guard did not sound the ceiling. "That way," said I to myself, "will lead me out of this place of torments." But for any such project to succeed I should have to depend purely on chance, for all my operations would leave visible traces. The cell was quite new, and the least scratch would have attracted the notice of my keepers.

I passed a terrible day, for the heat was like that of a furnace, and I was quite unable to make any use of the food with which I had been provided. The perspiration and the lack of nourishment made me so weak that I could neither walk nor read. Next day my dinner was the same; the horrible smell of the veal the rascal brought me made me draw back from it instantly. "Have you received orders," said I, "to kill me with hunger and heat?"

He locked the door, and went out without a word. On the third day I was treated in the same manner. I asked for a pencil and paper to write to the secretary. Still no answer.

In despair, I eat my soup, and then soaking my bread in a little Cyprus wine I resolved to get strength to avenge myself on Lawrence by plunging my pike into his throat. My rage told me that I had no other course, but I grew calmer in the night, and in the morning, when the scoundrel appeared, I contented myself with saying that I would kill him as soon as I was at liberty. He only laughed at my threat, and again went out without opening his lips.

I began to think that he was acting under orders from the secretary, to whom he must have told all. I knew not what to do. I strove between patience and despair, and felt as if I were dying for want of food. At last on the eighth day, with rage in my heart and in a voice of thunder, I bade him, under the name of "hangman," and in the presence of the archers, give me an account of my money. He answered drily that I should have it the next day. Then as he was about to go I took my bucket, and made as if I would go and empty it in the passage. Foreseeing my design, he told a guard to take it, and during the disgusting operation opened a window, which he shut as soon as the affair was done, so that in spite of my remonstrances I was left in the plague-stricken atmosphere. I determined to speak to him still worse the next day; but as soon as he appeared my anger cooled, for before giving me the account of my money he presented me with a basket of lemons which M. de Bragadin had sent me, also a large bottle of water, which seemed drinkable, and a nice roasted fowl; and, besides this, one of the guards opened the two windows. When he gave me the account I only looked at the sum total, and I told him to give the balance to his wife with the exception of a sequin, which I told him to give the guards who were with him. I thus made friends with these fellows, who thanked me heartily.

Lawrence, who remained alone with me on purpose, spoke as follows:

"You have already told me, sir, that I myself furnished you with the tools to make that enormous hole, and I will ask no more about it; but would you kindly tell me where you got the materials to make a lamp?"

"From you."

"Well, for the moment, sir, I'm dashed, for I did not think that wit meant impudence."

"I am not telling you any lies. You it was who with your own hands gave me all the requisites—oil, flint, and matches; the rest I had by me."

"You are right; but can you shew me as simply that I gave you the tools to make that hole?"

"Certainly, for you are the only person who has given me anything."

"Lord have mercy upon me! what do I hear? Tell me, then, how I gave you a hatchet?"

"I will tell you the whole story and I will speak the truth, but only in the presence of the secretary."

"I don't wish to know any more, and I believe everything you say. I only ask you to say nothing about it, as I am a poor man with a family to provide for." He went out with his head between his hands.

I congratulated myself heartily on having found a way to make the rascal afraid of me; he thought that I knew enough to hang him. I saw that his own interest would keep him from saying anything to his superiors about the matter.

I had told Lawrence to bring me the works of Maffei, but the expense displeased him though he did not dare to say so. He asked me what I could want with books with so many to my hand.

"I have read them all," I said, "and want some fresh ones."

"I will get someone who is here to lend you his books, if you will lend yours in return; thus you will save your money."

"Perhaps the books are romances, for which I do not care."

"They are scientific works; and if you think yours is the only long head here, you are very much mistaken."

"Very good, we shall see. I will lend this book to the 'long head,' and do you bring me one from him."

I had given him Petau's Rationarium, and in four minutes he brought me the first volume of Wolff's works. Well pleased with it I told him, much to his delight, that I would do without Maffei.

Less pleased with the learned reading than at the opportunity to begin a correspondence with someone who might help me in my plan of escape (which I had already sketched out in my head), I opened the book as soon as Lawrence was gone, and was overjoyed to find on one of the leaves the maxim of Seneca, "Calamitosus est animus futuri anxius," paraphrased in six elegant verses. I made another six on the spot, and this is the way in which I contrived to write them, I had let the nail of my little finger grow long to serve as an earpick; I out it to a point, and made a pen of it. I had no ink, and I was going to prick myself and write in my blood, when I bethought me that the juice of some mulberries I had by me would be an excellent substitute for ink. Besides the six verses I wrote out a list of my books, and put it in the back of the same book. It must be understood that Italian books are generally bound in parchment, and in such a way that when the book is opened the back becomes a kind of pocket. On the title page I wrote, "latet". I was anxious to get an answer, so the next day I told Lawrence that I had read the book and wanted another; and in a few minutes the second volume was in my hands.

As soon as I was alone I opened the book, and found a loose leaf with the following communication in Latin:

"Both of us are in the same prison, and to both of us it must be pleasant to find how the ignorance of our gaoler procures us a privilege before unknown to such a place. I, Marin Balbi, who write to you, am a Venetian of high birth, and a regular cleric, and my companion is Count Andre Asquin, of Udine, the capital of Friuli. He begs me to inform you that all the books in his possession, of which you will find a list at the back of this volume, are at your service; but we warn you that we must use all possible care to prevent our correspondence being discovered by Lawrence."

In our position there was nothing wonderful in our both pitching on the idea of sending each other the catalogues of our small libraries, or in our choosing the same hiding-place—the back of the books; all this was plain common sense; but the advice to be careful contained on the loose leaf struck me with some astonishment. It seemed next to impossible that Lawrence should leave the book unopened, but if he had opened it he would have seen the leaf, and not knowing how to read he would have kept it in his pocket till he could get someone to tell him the contents, and thus all would have been strangled at its birth. This made me think that my correspondent was an arrant block-head.

After reading through the list, I wrote who I was, how I had been arrested, my ignorance as to what crime I had committed, and my hope of soon becoming free. Balbi then wrote me a letter of sixteen pages, in which he gave me the history of all his misfortunes. He had been four years in prison, and the reason was that he had enjoyed the good graces of three girls, of whom he had three children, all of whom he baptized under his own name.

The first time his superior had let him off with an admonition, the second time he was threatened with punishment, and on the third and last occasion he was imprisoned. The father-superior of his convent brought him his dinner every day. He told me in his letter that both the superior and the Tribunal were tyrants, since they had no lawful authority over his conscience: that being sure that the three children were his, he thought himself constrained as a man of honour not to deprive them of the advantage of bearing his name. He finished by telling me that he had found himself obliged to recognize his children to prevent slander attributing them to others, which would have injured the reputation of the three honest girls who bore them; and besides he could not stifle the voice of nature, which spoke so well on behalf of these little ones. His last words were, "There is no danger of the superior falling into the same fault, as he confines his attention to the boys."

This letter made me know my man. Eccentric, sensual, a bad logician, vicious, a fool, indiscreet, and ungrateful, all this appeared in his letter, for after telling me that he should be badly off without Count Asquin who was seventy years old, and had books and money, he devoted two pages to abusing him, telling me of his faults and follies. In society I should have had nothing more to do with a man of his character, but under the Leads I was obliged to put everything to some use. I found in the back of the book a pencil, pens, and paper, and I was thus enabled to write at my ease.

He told me also the history of the prisoners who were under the Leads, and of those who had been there since his imprisonment. He said that the guard who secretly brought him whatever he wanted was called Nicolas, he also told me the names of the prisoners, and what he knew about them, and to convince me he gave me the history of the hole I had made. It seems I had been taken from my cell to make room for the patrician Priuli, and that Lawrence had taken two hours to repair the damage I had done, and that he had imparted the secret to the carpenter, the blacksmith, and all the guards under pain of death if they revealed it. "In another day," the guard had said, "Casanova would have escaped, and Lawrence would have swung, for though he pretended great astonishment when he saw the hole, there can be no doubt that he and no other provided the tools." "Nicolas has told me," added my correspondent, "that M. de Bragadin has promised him a thousand sequins if he will aid you to make your escape but that Lawrence, who knows of it, hopes to get the money without risking his neck, his plan being to obtain your liberty by means of the influence of his wife with M. Diedo. None of the guards dare to speak of what happened for fear Lawrence might get himself out of the difficulty, and take his revenge by having them dismissed." He begged me to tell him all the details, and how I got the tools, and to count upon his keeping the secret.

I had no doubts as to his curiosity, but many as to his discretion, and this very request shewed him to be the most indiscreet of men. Nevertheless, I concluded that I must make use of him, for he seemed to me the kind of man to assist me in my escape. I began to write an answer to him, but a sudden suspicion made me keep back what I had written. I fancied that the correspondence might be a mere artifice of Lawrence's to find out who had given me the tools, and what I had done with them. To satisfy him without compromising myself I told him that I had made the hole with a strong knife in my possession, which I had placed on the window-ledge in the passage. In less than three days this false confidence of mine made me feel secure, as Lawrence did not go to the window, as he would certainly have done if the letter had been intercepted. Furthermore, Father Balbi told me that he could understand how I might have a knife, as Lawrence had told him that I had not been searched previous to my imprisonment. Lawrence himself had received no orders to search me, and this circumstance might have stood him in good stead if I had succeeded in escaping, as all prisoners handed over to him by the captain of the guard were supposed to have been searched already. On the other hand, Messer-Grande might have said that, having seen me get out of my bed, he was sure that I had no weapons about me, and thus both of them would have got out of trouble. The monk ended by begging me to send him my knife by Nicolas, on whom I might rely.

The monk's thoughtlessness seemed to me almost incredible. I wrote and told him that I was not at all inclined to put my trust in Nicolas, and that my secret was one not to be imparted in writing. However, I was amused by his letters. In one of them he told me why Count Asquin was kept under the Leads, in spite of his helplessness, for he was enormously fat, and as he had a broken leg which had been badly set he could hardly put one foot before another. It seems that the count, not being a very wealthy man, followed the profession of a barrister at Udine, and in that capacity defended the country-folk against the nobility, who wished to deprive the peasants of their vote in the assembly of the province. The claims of the farmers disturbed the public peace, and by way of bringing them to reason the nobles had recourse to the State Inquisitors, who ordered the count-barrister to abandon his clients. The count replied that the municipal law authorized him to defend the constitution, and would not give in; whereon the Inquisitors arrested him, law or no law, and for the last five years he had breathed the invigorating air of The Leads. Like myself he had fifty sous a day, but he could do what he liked with the money. The monk, who was always penniless, told me a good deal to the disadvantage of the count, whom he represented as very miserly. He informed me that in the cell on the other side of the hall there were two gentlemen of the "Seven Townships," who were likewise imprisoned for disobedience, but one of them had become mad, and was in chains; in another cell, he said, there were two lawyers.

My suspicions quieted, I reasoned as follows:

I wish to regain my liberty at all hazards. My pike is an admirable instrument, but I can make no use of it as my cell is sounded all over (except the ceiling) every day. If I would escape, it is by the ceiling, therefore, that way I must go, but to do that I must make a hole through it, and that I cannot do from my side, for it would not be the work of a day. I must have someone to help me; and not having much choice I had to pick out the monk. He was thirty-eight, and though not rich in common sense I judged that the love of liberty—the first need of man—would give him sufficient courage to carry out any orders I might give. I must begin by telling him my plan in its entirety, and then I shall have to find a way to give him the bar. I had, then, two difficult problems before me.

My first step was to ask him if he wished to be free, and if he were disposed to hazard all in attempting his escape in my company. He replied that his mate and he would do anything to break their chains, but, added he, "it is of no use to break one's head against a stone wall." He filled four pages with the impossibilities which presented themselves to his feeble intellect, for the fellow saw no chance of success on any quarter. I replied that I did not trouble myself with general difficulties, and that in forming my plan I had only thought of special difficulties, which I would find means to overcome, and I finished by giving him my word of honour to set him free, if he would promise to carry out exactly whatever orders I might give.

He gave me his promise to do so. I told him that I had a pike twenty inches long, and with this tool he must pierce the ceiling of his cell next the wall which separated us, and he would then be above my head; his next step would be to make a hole in the ceiling of my cell and aid me to escape by it. "Here your task will end and mine will begin, and I will undertake to set both you and Count Asquin at liberty."

He answered that when I had got out of my cell I should be still in prison, and our position would be the same as now, as we should only be in the garrets which were secured by three strong doors.

"I know that, reverend father," I replied, "but we are not going to escape by the doors. My plan is complete, and I will guarantee its success. All I ask of you is to carry out my directions, and to make no difficulties. Do you busy yourself to find out some way of getting my bar without the knowledge of the gaoler. In the meanwhile, make him get you about forty pictures of saints, large enough to cover all the walls of your cell. Lawrence will suspect nothing, and they will do to conceal the opening you are to make in the ceiling. To do this will be the work of some days, and of mornings Lawrence will not see what you have done the day before, as you will have covered it up with one of the pictures. If you ask me why I do not undertake the work myself, I can only say that the gaoler suspects me, and the objection will doubtless seem to you a weighty one."

Although I had told him to think of a plan to get hold of the pike, I thought of nothing else myself, and had a happy thought which I hastened to put into execution. I told Lawrence to buy me a folio Bible, which had been published recently; it was the Vulgate with the Septuagint. I hoped to be able to put the pike in the back of the binding of this large volume, and thus to convey it to the monk, but when I saw the book I found the tool to be two inches longer.

My correspondent had written to tell me that his cell was covered with pictures, and I had communicated him my idea about the Bible and the difficulty presented by its want of length. Happy at being able to display his genius, he rallied me on the poverty of my imagination, telling me that I had only to send him the pike wrapped up in my fox-skin cloak.

"Lawrence," said he, "had often talked about your cloak, and Count Asquin would arouse no suspicion by asking to see it in order to buy one of the same kind. All you have to do is to send it folded up. Lawrence would never dream of unfolding it."

I, on the other hand, was sure that he would. In the first place, because a cloak folded up is more troublesome to carry than when it is unfolded. However, not to rebuff him and at the same time to shew him that I was the wiser, I wrote that he had only to send for the cloak. The next day Lawrence asked me for it, and I gave it folded up, but without the bar, and in a quarter of an hour he brought it back to me, saying that the gentleman had admired it very much.

The monk wrote me a doleful letter, in which he confessed he had given me a piece of bad advice, adding that I was wrong to follow it. According to him the pike was lost, as Lawrence had brought in the cloak all unfolded. After this, all hope was gone. I undeceived him, and begged him for the future to be a little more sparing of his advice. It was necessary to bring the matter to a head, and I determined to send him the bar under cover of my Bible, taking measures to prevent the gaoler from seeing the ends of the great volume. My scheme was as follows:

I told Lawrence that I wanted to celebrate St. Michael's Day with a macaroni cheese; but wishing to shew my gratitude to the person who had kindly lent me his books, I should like to make him a large dish of it, and to prepare it with my own hands. Lawrence told me (as had been arranged between the monk and myself) that the gentleman in question wished to read the large book which cost three sequins.

"Very good," said I, "I will send it him with the macaroni; but get me the largest dish you have, as I wish to do the thing on a grand scale."

He promised to do what I asked him. I wrapped up the pike in paper and put it in the back of the Bible, taking care that it projected an equal distance at each end. Now, if I placed on the Bible a great dish of macaroni full of melted butter I was quite sure that Lawrence would not examine the ends. All his gaze would be concentrated upon the plate, to avoid spilling the grease on the book. I told Father Balbi of my plan, charging him to take care how he took the dish, and above all to take dish and Bible together, and not one by one. On the day appointed Lawrence came earlier than usual, carrying a saucepan full of boiling macaroni, and all the necessary ingredients for seasoning the dish. I melted a quantity of butter, and after putting the macaroni into the dish I poured the butter over it till it was full to the brim. The dish was a huge one, and was much larger than the book on which I placed it. I did all this at the door of my cell, Lawrence being outside.

When all was ready I carefully took up the Bible and dish, placing the back of the book next to the bearer, and told Lawrence to stretch out his arms and take it, to be careful not to spill the grease over the book, and to carry the whole to its destination immediately. As I gave him this weighty load I kept my eyes fixed on his, and I saw to my joy that he did not take his gaze off the butter, which he was afraid of spilling. He said it would be better to take the dish first, and then to come back for the book; but I told him that this would spoil the present, and that both must go together. He then complained that I had put in too much butter, and said, jokingly, that if it were spilt he would not be responsible for the loss. As soon as I saw the Bible in the lout's arms I was certain of success, as he could not see the ends of the pike without twisting his head, and I saw no reason why he should divert his gaze from the plate, which he had enough to do to carry evenly. I followed him with my eyes till he disappeared into the ante-chamber of the monk's cell, and he, blowing his nose three times, gave me the pre-arranged signal that all was right, which was confirmed by the appearance of Lawrence in a few moments afterwards.

Father Balbi lost no time in setting about the work, and in eight days he succeeded in making a large enough opening in the ceiling, which he covered with a picture pasted to the ceiling with breadcrumbs. On the 8th of October he wrote to say that he had passed the whole night in working at the partition wall, and had only succeeded in loosening one brick. He told me the difficulty of separating the bricks joined to one another by a strong cement was enormous, but he promised to persevere, "though," he said, "we shall only make our position worse than it is now." I told him that I was certain of success; that he must believe in me and persevere. Alas! I was certain of nothing, but I had to speak thus or to give up all. I was fain to escape from this hell on earth, where I was imprisoned by a most detestable tyranny, and I thought only of forwarding this end, with the resolve to succeed, or at all events not to stop before I came to a difficulty which was insurmountable. I had read in the great book of experience that in important schemes action is the grand requisite, and that the rest must be left to fortune. If I had entrusted Father Balbi with these deep mysteries of moral philosophy he would have pronounced me a madman. His work was only toilsome on the first night, for the more he worked the easier it became, and when he had finished he found he had taken out thirty-six bricks.

On the 16th of October, as I was engaged in translating an ode of Horace, I heard a trampling noise above my head, and then three light blows were struck. This was the signal agreed upon to assure us that our calculations were correct. He worked till the evening, and the next day he wrote that if the roof of my cell was only two boards thick his work would be finished that day. He assured me that he was carefully making the hole round as I had charged him, and that he would not pierce the ceiling. This was a vital point, as the slightest mark would have led to discovery. "The final touch," he said, "will only take a quarter of an hour." I had fixed on the day after the next to escape from my cell at night-time to enter no more, for with a mate I was quite sure that I could make in two or three hours a hole in the roof of the ducal palace, and once on the outside of the roof I would trust to chance for the means of getting to the ground.

I had not yet got so far as this, for my bad luck had more than one obstacle in store for me. On the same day (it was a Monday) at two o'clock in the afternoon, whilst Father Balbi was at work, I heard the door of the hall being opened. My blood ran cold, but I had sufficient presence of mind to knock twice-the signal of alarm—at which it had been agreed that Father Balbi was to make haste back to his cell and set all in order. In less than a minute afterwards Lawrence opened the door, and begged my pardon for giving me a very unpleasant companion. This was a man between forty and fifty, short, thin, ugly, and badly dressed, wearing a black wig; while I was looking at him he was unbound by two guards. I had no reason to doubt that he was a knave, since Lawrence told me so before his face without his displaying the slightest emotion. "The Court," I said, "can do what seems good to it." After Lawrence had brought him a bed he told him that the Court allowed him ten sous a day, and then locked us up together.

Overwhelmed by this disaster, I glanced at the fellow, whom his every feature proclaimed rogue. I was about to speak to him when he began by thanking me for having got him a bed. Wishing to gain him over, I invited him to take his meals with me. He kissed my hand, and asked me if he would still be able to claim the ten sous which the Court had allowed him. On my answering in the affirmative he fell on his knees, and drawing an enormous rosary from his pocket he cast his gaze all round the cell.

"What do you want?"

"You will pardon me, sir, but I am looking for some statue of the Holy Virgin, for I am a Christian; if there were even a small crucifix it would be something, for I have never been in so much need of the protection of St. Francis d'Assisi, whose name I bear, though all unworthy."

I could scarcely help laughing, not at his Christian piety, since faith and conscience are beyond control, but at the curious turn he gave his remonstrance. I concluded he took me for a Jew; and to disabuse him of this notion I made haste to give him the "Hours of the Holy Virgin," whose picture he kissed, and then gave me the book back, telling me in a modest voice that his father—a galley officer—had neglected to have him taught to read. "I am," said he, "a devotee of the Holy Rosary," and he told me a host of miracles, to which I listened with the patience of an angel. When he had come to an end I asked him if he had had his dinner, and he replied that he was dying of hunger. I gave him everything I had, which he devoured rather than ate; drinking all my wine, and then becoming maudlin he began to weep, and finally to talk without rhyme or reason. I asked him how he got into trouble, and he told me the following story:

"My aim and my only aim has always been the glory of God, and of the holy Republic of Venice, and that its laws may be exactly obeyed. Always lending an attentive ear to the plots of the wicked, whose end is to deceive, to deprive their prince of his just dues, and to conspire secretly, I have over and again unveiled their secret plans, and have not failed to report to Messer-Grande all I know. It is true that I am always paid, but the money has never given me so much pleasure as the thought that I have been able to serve the blessed St. Mark. I have always despised those who think there is something dishonourable in the business of a spy. The word sounds ill only to the ill-affected; for a spy is a lover of the state, the scourge of the guilty, and faithful subject of his prince. When I have been put to the test, the feeling of friendship, which might count for something with other men, has never had the slightest influence over me, and still less the sentiment which is called gratitude. I have often, in order to worm out a secret, sworn to be as silent as the grave, and have never failed to reveal it. Indeed, I am able to do so with full confidence, as my director who is a good Jesuit has told me that I may lawfully reveal such secrets, not only because my intention was to do so, but because, when the safety of the state is at stake, there is no such thing as a binding oath. I must confess that in my zeal I have betrayed my own father, and that in me the promptings of our weak nature have been quite mortified. Three weeks ago I observed that there was a kind of cabal between four or five notables of the town of Isola, where I live. I knew them to be disaffected to the Government on account of certain contraband articles which had been confiscated. The first chaplain—a subject of Austria by birth—was in the plot. They gathered together of evenings in an inn, in a room where there was a bed; there they drank and talked, and afterwards went their ways. As I was determined to discover the conspiracy, I was brave enough to hide under the bed on a day on which I was sure I would not be seen. Towards the evening my gentlemen came, and began to talk; amongst other things, they said that the town of Isola was not within the jurisdiction of St. Mark, but rather in the principality of Trieste, as it could not possibly be considered to form part of the Venetian territory. The chaplain said to the chief of the plot, a man named Pietro Paolo, that if he and the others would sign a document to that effect, he himself would go to the imperial ambassador, and that the Empress would not only take possession of the island, but would reward them for what they had done. They all professed themselves ready to go on, and the chaplain promised to bring the document the next day, and afterwards to take it to the ambassadors.

"I determined to frustrate this detestable project, although one of the conspirators was my gossip—a spiritual relationship which gave him a greater claim on me than if he had been my own brother.

"After they were gone, I came out of my hiding-place and did not think it necessary to expose myself to danger by hiding again as I had found out sufficient for my purpose. I set out the same night in a boat, and reached here the next day before noon. I had the names of the six rebels written down, and I took the paper to the secretary of the Tribunal, telling him all I had heard. He ordered me to appear, the day following, at the palace, and an agent of the Government should go back with me to Isola that I might point the chaplain out to him, as he had probably not yet gone to the Austrian ambassador's. 'That done,' said the lord secretary, 'you will no longer meddle in the matter.' I executed his orders, and after having shewn the chaplain to the agent, I was at leisure for my own affairs.

"After dinner my gossip called me in to shave him (for I am a barber by profession), and after I had done so he gave me a capital glass of refosco with some slices of sausages, and we ate together in all good fellowship. My love for him had still possession of my soul, so I took his hand, and, shedding some heartfelt tears, I advised him to have no more to do with the canon, and above all, not to sign the document he knew of. He protested that he was no particular friend of the chaplain's, and swore he did not know what document I was talking about. I burst into a laugh, telling him it was only my joke, and went forth very sorry at having yielded to a sentiment of affection which had made me commit so grievous a fault. The next day I saw neither the man nor the chaplain. A week after, having paid a visit to the palace, I was promptly imprisoned, and here I am with you, my dear sir. I thank St. Francis for having given me the company of a good Christian, who is here for reasons of which I desire to know nothing, for I am not curious. My name is Soradaci, and my wife is a Legrenzi, daughter of a secretary to the Council of Ten, who, in spite of all prejudice to the contrary, determined to marry me. She will be in despair at not knowing what has become of me, but I hope to be here only for a few days, since the only reason of my imprisonment is that the secretary wishes to be able to examine me more conveniently."

I shuddered to think of the monster who was with me, but feeling that the situation was a risky one, And that I should have to make use of him, I compassionated him, praised his patriotism, and predicted that he would be set at liberty in a few days. A few moments after he fell asleep, and I took the opportunity of telling the whole story to Father Balbi, shewing him that we should be obliged to put off our work to a more convenient season. Next day I told Lawrence to buy me a wooden crucifix, a statue of Our Lady, a portrait of St. Francis, and two bottles of holy water. Soradaci asked for his ten sous, and Lawrence, with an air of contempt, gave him twenty. I asked Lawrence to buy me four times the usual amount of garlic, wine, and salt—a diet in which my hateful companion delighted. After the gaoler was gone I deftly drew out the letter Balbi had written me, and in which he drew a vivid picture of his alarm. He thought all was lost, and over and over again thanked Heaven that Lawrence had put Soradaci in my cell, "for," said he, "if he had come into mine, he would not have found me there, and we should possibly have shared a cell in The Wells as a reward for our endeavours."

Soradaci's tale had satisfied me that he was only imprisoned to be examined, as it seemed plain that the secretary had arrested him on suspicion of bearing false witness. I thereupon resolved to entrust him with two letters which would do me neither good nor harm if they were delivered at their addresses, but which would be beneficial to me if the traitor gave them to the secretary as a proof of his loyalty, as I had not the slightest doubt he would do.

I spent two hours in writing these two letters in pencil. Next day Lawrence brought me the crucifix, the two pictures, and the holy water, and having worked the rascal well up to the point, I said, "I reckon upon your friendship and your courage. Here are two letters I want you to deliver when you recover your liberty. My happiness depends on your loyalty, but you must hide the letters, as they were found upon you we should both of us be undone. You must swear by the crucifix and these holy pictures not to betray me."

"I am ready, dear master, to swear to anything you like, and I owe you too much to betray you."

This speech was followed by much weeping and lamentation. He called himself unhappy wretch at being suspected of treason towards a man for whom he would have given his life. I knew my man, but I played out the comedy. Having given him a shirt and a cap, I stood up bare-headed, and then having sprinkled the cell with holy water, and plentifully bedewed him with the same liquid, I made him swear a dreadful oath, stuffed with senseless imprecations, which for that very reason were the better fitted to strike terror to his soul. After his having sworn the oath to deliver my letters to their addresses, I gave him them, and he himself proposed to sew them up at the back of his waistcoat, between the stuff and the lining, to which proceedings I assented.

I was morally sure that he would deliver my letters to the secretary in the first opportunity, so I took the utmost care that my style of writing should not discover the trick. They could only gain me the esteem of the Court, and possibly its mercy. One of the letters was addressed to M. de Bragadin and the other to the Abbe Grimani, and I told them not to be anxious about me as I was in good hopes of soon being set at liberty, that they would find when I came out that my imprisonment had done me more good than harm, as there was no one in Venice who stood in need of reform more than I.

I begged M. de Bragadin to be kind enough to send me a pair of fur boots for the winter, as my cell was high enough for me to stand upright and to walk up and down.

I took care that Soradaci should not suspect the innocent nature of these letters, as he might then have been seized with the temptation to do an honest thing for me, and have delivered them, which was not what I was aiming at. You will see, dear reader, in the following chapter, the power of oaths over the vile soul of my odious companion, and also if I have not verified the saying 'In vino veritas', for in the story he told me the wretch had shewn himself in his true colours.

IV

TREASON OF SORADACI—HOW I GET THE BEST OF HIM—
FATHER BALBI ENDS HIS WORK—I ESCAPE FROM MY
CELL—UNSEASONABLE OBSERVATIONS OF COUNT
ASQUIN THE CRITICAL MOMENT

Soradaci had had my letters for two or three days when Lawrence came one afternoon to take him to the secretary. As he was several hours away, I hoped to see his face no more; but to my great astonishment he was brought back in the evening. As soon as Lawrence had gone, he told me that the secretary suspected him of having warned the chaplain, since that individual had never been near the ambassador's and no document of any kind was found upon him. He added that after a long examination he had been confined in a very small cell, and was then bound and brought again before the secretary, who wanted him to confess that he told someone at Isola that the priest would never return, but that he had not done so as he had said no such thing. At last the secretary got tired, called the guards, and had him brought back to my cell.

I was distressed to hear his account, as I saw that the wretch would probably remain a long time in my company. Having to inform Father Balbi of this fatal misadventure, I wrote to him during the night, and being obliged to do so more than once, I got accustomed to write correctly enough in the dark.

On the next day, to assure myself that my suspicions were well founded, I told the spy to give me the letter I had written to M. de Bragadin as I wanted to add something to it. "You can sew it up afterwards," said I.

"It would be dangerous," he replied, "as the gaoler might come in in the mean time, and then we should be both ruined."

"No matter. Give me my letters:"

Thereupon the hound threw himself at my feet, and swore that on his appearing for a second time before the dreaded secretary, he had been seized with a severe trembling; and that he had felt in his back, especially in the place where the letters were, so intolerable an oppression, that the secretary had asked him the cause, and that he had not been able to conceal the truth. Then the secretary rang his bell, and Lawrence came in, unbound him, and took off his waist-coat and unsewed the lining. The secretary then read the letters and put them in a drawer of his bureau, telling him that if he had taken the letters he would have been discovered and have lost his life.

I pretended to be overwhelmed, and covering my face with my hands I knelt down at the bedside before the picture of the Virgin, and asked, her to avenge me on the wretch who had broken the most sacred oaths. I afterwards lay down on the bed, my face to the wall, and remained there the whole day without moving, without speaking a word, and pretending not to hear the tears, cries, and protestations of repentance uttered by the villain. I played my part in the comedy I had sketched out to perfection. In the night I wrote to Father Balbi to come at two o'clock in the afternoon, not a minute sooner or later, to work for four hours, and not a minute more. "On this precision," I wrote, "our liberty depends and if you observe it all will be well."

It was the 25th of October, and the time for me to carry out my design or to give it up for ever drew near. The State Inquisitors and their secretary went every year to a village on the mainland, and passed there the first three days of November. Lawrence, taking advantage of his masters' absence, did not fail to get drunk every evening, and did not appear at The Leads in the morning till a late hour.

Advised of these circumstances, I chose this time to make my escape, as I was certain that my flight would not be noticed till late in the morning. Another reason for my determination to hurry my escape, when I could no longer doubt the villainy of my detestable companion, seems to me to be worthy of record.

The greatest relief of a man in the midst of misfortune is the hope of escaping from it. He sighs for the hour when his sorrows are to end; he thinks he can hasten it by his prayers; he will do anything to know when his torments shall cease. The sufferer, impatient and enfeebled, is mostly inclined to superstition. "God," says he, "knows the time, and God may reveal it to me, it matters not how." Whilst he is in this state he is ready to trust in divination in any manner his fancy leads him, and is more or less disposed to believe in the oracle of which he makes choice.

I then was in this state of mind; but not knowing how to make use of the Bible to inform me of the moment in which I should recover my liberty, I determined to consult the divine Orlando Furioso, which I had read a hundred times, which I knew by heart, and which was my delight under the Leads. I idolized the genius of Ariosto, and considered him a far better fortune-teller than Virgil.

With this idea I wrote a question addressed to the supposed Intelligence, in which I ask in what canto of Ariosto I should find the day of my deliverance. I then made a reversed pyramid composed of the number formed from the words of the question, and by subtracting the number nine I obtained, finally, nine. This told me that I should find my fate in the ninth canto. I followed the same method to find out the exact stanza and verse, and got seven for the stanza and one for the verse.

I took up the poem, and my heart beating as if I trusted wholly in the oracle, I opened it, turned down the leaf, and read;

'Fra il fin d'ottobre, a il capo di novembre'.

The precision of the line and its appropriateness to my circumstances appeared so wonderful to me, that I will not confess that I placed my faith entirely in it; but the reader will pardon me if I say that I did all in my power to make the prediction a correct one. The most singular circumstance is that between the end of October and the beginning of November, there is only the instant midnight, and it was just as the clock was striking midnight on the 31st of October that I escaped from my cell, as the reader will soon see.

The following is the manner in which I passed the morning to strike awe into the soul of that vicious brute, to confound his feeble intellect, and to render him harmless to me.

As soon as Lawrence had left us I told Soradaci to come and take some soup. The scoundrel was in bed, and he had told Lawrence that he was ill. He would not have dared to approach me if I had not called him. However, he rose from his bed, and threw himself flat upon the ground at my feet, and said, weeping violently, that if I would not forgive him he would die before the day was done, as he already felt the curse and the vengeance of the Holy Virgin which I had denounced against him. He felt devouring pains in his bowels, and his mouth was covered with sores. He shewed it me, and I saw it was full of ulcers, but I cannot say whether it was thus the night before. I did not much care to examine him to see if he were telling me the truth. My cue was to pretend to believe him, and to make him hope for mercy. I began by making him eat and drink. The traitor most likely intended to deceive me, but as I was myself determined to deceive him it remained to be seen which was the a cuter. I had planned an attack against which it was improbable that he could defend himself.

Assuming an inspired air, I said, "Be seated and take this soup, and afterwards I will tell you of your good fortune, for know that the Virgin of the Rosary appeared to me at day-break, and bids me pardon you. Thou shalt not die but live, and shalt come out of this place with me." In great wonderment, and kneeling on the ground for want of a chair, he ate the soup with me, and afterwards seated himself on the bed to hear what I had to say. Thus I spoke to him:

"The grief I experienced at your dreadful treason made me pass a sleepless night, as the letters might condemn me to spend here the remnant of my days. My only consolation, I confess, was the certainty that you would die here also before my eyes within three days. Full of this thought not worthy of a Christian (for God bids us forgive our enemies) my weariness made me sleep, and in my sleep I had a vision. I saw that Holy Virgin, Mother of God, whose likeness you behold—I saw her before me, and opening her lips she spoke thus:

"'Soradaci is a devotee of my Holy Rosary. I protect him, and I will that you forgive him, and then the curse he has drawn on himself will cease. In return for your generosity, I will order one of my angels to take the form of man, to come down from heaven, to break open the roof of your prison, and set you free within five or six days. The angel will begin his task this day at two o'clock precisely, and he will work till half an hour before sunset, since he must ascend again into heaven while the daylight lasts. When you come out of this place, take Soradaci with you, and have a care for him if he will renounce his business of spying. Tell him all.'

"With these words the Holy Virgin vanished out of my sight, and I awoke."

I spoke all the while with a serious face and the air of one inspired, and I saw that the traitor was petrified. I then took my Book of Hours, sprinkled the cell with holy water, and pretended to pray, kissing from time to time the picture of the Virgin. An hour afterwards the brute, who so far had not opened his mouth, asked me bluntly at what time the angel would come down from heaven, and if we should hear him breaking in the cell.

"I am certain that he will begin at two o'clock, that we shall hear him at his work, and that he will depart at the hour named by the Holy Virgin."

"You may have dreamt it all."

"Nay, not so. Will you swear to me to spy no more?"

Instead of answering he went off to sleep, and did not awake for two hours after, when he asked if he could put off taking the oath. I asked of him,

"You can put off taking it," I said, "till the angel enters to set me free; but if you do not then renounce by an oath the infamous trade which has brought you here, and which will end by bringing you to the gallows, I shall leave you in the cell, for so the Mother of God commands, and if you do not obey you will lose her protection."

As I had expected, I saw an expression of satisfaction on his hideous features, for he was quite certain that the angel would not come. He looked at me with a pitying air. I longed to hear the hour strike. The play amused me intensely, for I was persuaded that the approach of the angel would set his miserable wits a-reeling. I was sure, also, that the plan would succeed if Lawrence had not forgotten to give the monk the books, and this was not likely.

An hour before the time appointed I was fain to dine. I only drank water, and Soradaci drank all the wine and consumed all the garlic I had, and thus made himself worse.

As soon as I heard the first stroke of two I fell on my knees, ordering him, in an awful voice, to do the like. He obeyed, looking at me in a dazed way. When I heard the first slight noise I examined, "Lo! the angel cometh!" and fell down on my face, and with a hearty fisticuff forced him into the same position. The noise of breaking was plainly heard, and for a quarter of an hour I kept in that troublesome position, and if the circumstances had been different I should have laughed to see how motionless the creature was; but I restrained myself, remembering my design of completely turning the fellow's head, or at least of obsessing him for a time. As soon as I got up I knelt and allowed him to imitate me, and I spent three hours in saying the rosary to him. From time to time he dozed off, wearied rather by his position than by the monotony of the prayer, but during the whole time he never interrupted me. Now and again he dared to raise a furtive glance towards the ceiling. With a sort of stupor on his face, he turned his head in the direction of the Virgin, and the whole of his behaviour was for me the highest comedy. When I heard the clock strike the hour for the work to cease, I said to him,

"Prostrate thyself, for the angel departeth."

Balbi returned to his cell, and we heard him no more. As I rose to my feet, fixing my gaze on the wretched fellow, I read fright on every feature, and was delighted. I addressed a few words to him that I might see in what state of mind he was. He shed tears in abundance, and what he said was mostly extravagant, his ideas having no sequence or connection. He spoke of his sins, of his acts of devotion, of his zeal in the service of St. Mark, and of the work he had done for the Commonwealth, and to this attributed the special favours Mary had shewn him. I had to put up with a long story about the miracles of the Rosary which his wife, whose confessor was a young Dominican, had told him. He said that he did not know what use I could make of an ignorant fellow like him.

"I will take you into my service, and you shall have all that you need without being obliged to pursue the hazardous trade of a spy."

"Shall we not be able to remain at Venice?"

"Certainly not. The angel will take us to a land which does not belong to St. Mark. Will you swear to me that you will spy no more? And if you swear, will you become a perjurer a second time?"

"If I take the oath, I will surely keep it, of that there can be no doubt; but you must confess that if I had not perjured myself you would never have received such favour at the hands of the Virgin. My broken faith is the cause of your bliss. You ought, therefore, to love me and to be content with my treason."

"Dost love Judas who betrayed Jesus Christ?"

"No."

"You perceive, then, that one detests the traitor and at the same time adores the Divine Providence, which knows how to bring good out of evil. Up to the present time you have done wickedly. You have offended God and the Virgin His Mother, and I will not receive your oath till you have expiated your sins."

"What sin have I done?"

"You have sinned by pride, Soradaci, in thinking that I was under an obligation to you for betraying me and giving my letters to the secretary."

"How shall I expiate this sin?"

"Thus. To-morrow, when Lawrence comes, you must lie on your bed, your face towards the wall, and without the slightest motion or a single glance at Lawrence. If he address you, you must answer, without looking at him, that you could not sleep, and need rest. Do you promise me entirely to do this thing?"

"I will do whatsoever you tell me."

"Quick, then, take your oath before this holy picture."

"I promise, Holy Mother of God, that when Lawrence comes I will not look at him, nor stir from my bed."

"And I, Most Holy Virgin, swear by the bowels of your Divine Son that if I see Soradici move in the least or look towards Lawrence, I will throw myself straightway upon him and strangle him without mercy, to your honour and glory."

I counted on my threat having at least as much effect upon him as his oath. Nevertheless, as I was anxious to make sure, I asked him if he had anything to say against the oath, and after thinking for a moment he answered that he was quite content with it. Well pleased myself, I gave him something to eat, and told him to go to bed as I needed sleep.

As soon as he was asleep I began to write, and wrote on for two hours. I told Balbi all that had happened, and said that if the work was far enough advanced he need only come above my cell to put the final stroke to it and break through. I made him note that we should set out on the night of the 31st of October, and that we should be four in all, counting his companion and mine. It was now the twenty-eighth of the month.

In the morning the monk wrote me that the passage was made, and that he should only require to work at the ceiling of my cell to break through the last board and this would be done in four minutes. Soradaci observed his oath, pretending to sleep, and Lawrence said nothing to him. I kept my eyes upon him the whole time, and I verily believe I should have strangled him if he had made the slightest motion towards Lawrence, for a wink would have been enough to betray me.

The rest of the day was devoted to high discourses and exalted expressions, which I uttered as solemnly as I could, and I enjoyed the sight of seeing him become more and more fanatical. To heighten the effect of my mystic exhortation I dosed him heavily with wine, and did not let him go till he had fallen into a drunken sleep.

Though a stranger to all metaphysical speculations, and a man who had never exercised his reasoning faculties except in devising some piece of spy-craft, the fellow confused me for a moment by saying that he could not conceive how an angel should have to take so much trouble to break open our cell. But after lifting my eyes to heaven, or rather to the roof of my dungeon-cell, I said,

"The ways of God are inscrutable; and since the messenger of Heaven works not as an angel (for then a slight single blow would be enough), he works like a man, whose form he has doubtless taken, as we are not worthy to look upon his celestial body. And, furthermore," said I, like a true Jesuit, who knows how to draw advantage from everything, "I foresee that the angel, to punish us for your evil thought, which has offended the Holy Virgin, will not come to-day. Wretch, your thoughts are not those of an honest, pious, and religious man, but those of a sinner who thinks he has to do with Messer-Grande and his myrmidons."

I wanted to drive him to despair, and I had succeeded. He began to weep bitterly, and his sobs almost choked him, when two o'clock struck and not sign of the angel was heard. Instead of calming him I endeavoured to augment his misery by my complaints. The next morning he was obedient to my orders, for when Lawrence asked him how he was, he replied without moving his head. He behaved in the same manner on the day following, and until I saw Lawrence for the last time on the morning of the 31st October. I gave him the book for Barbi, and told the monk to come at noon to break through the ceiling. I feared nothing, as Lawrence had told me that the Inquisitors and the secretary had already set out for the country. I had no reason to dread the arrival of a new companion, and all I had to do was to manage my knave.

After Lawrence was gone I told Soradaci that the angel would come and make an opening in the ceiling about noon.

"He will bring a pair of scissors with him," I said, "and you will have to cut the angel's beard and mine."

"Has the angel a beard?"

"Yes, you shall see it for yourself. Afterwards we will get out of the cell and proceed to break the roof of the palace, whence we shall descend into St. Mark's Place and set out for Germany."

He answered nothing. He had to eat by himself, for my mind was too much occupied to think about dinner—indeed, I had been unable to sleep.

The appointed hour struck—and the angel came, Soradaci was going to fall down on his face, but I told him it was not necessary. In three minutes the passage was completed, the piece of board fell at my feet, and Father Balbi into my arms. "Your work is ended and mine begun," said I to him. We embraced each other, and he gave me the pike and a pair of scissors. I told Soradaci to cut our beards, but I could not help laughing to see the creature—his mouth all agape-staring at the angel, who was more like a devil. However, though quite beside himself, he cut our beards admirably.

Anxious to see how the land lay, I told the monk to stay with Soradaci, as I did not care to leave him alone, and I went out. I found the hole in the wall narrow, but I succeeded in getting through it. I was above the count's cell, and I came in and greeted the worthy old man. The man before me was not fitted to encounter such difficulties as would be involved in an escape by a steep roof covered with plates of lead. He asked me what my plan was, and told me that he thought I had acted rather inconsiderately. "I only ask to go forward," said I, "till I find death or freedom." "If you intend," he answered, "to pierce the roof and to descend from thence, I see no prospect of success, unless you have wings; and I at all events have not the courage to accompany you. I will remain here, and pray to God on your behalf."

I went out again to look at the roof, getting as close as I could to the sides of the loft. Touching the lower part of the roof, I took up a position between the beams, and feeling the wood with the end of the bar I luckily found them to be half rotten. At every blow of the bar they fell to dust, so feeling certain of my ability to make a large enough hole in less than a hour I returned to my cell, and for four hours employed myself in cutting up sheets, coverlets, and bedding, to make ropes. I took care to make the knots myself and to be assured of their strength, for a single weak knot might cost us our lives. At last I had ready a hundred fathoms of rope.

In great undertakings there are certain critical points which the leader who deserves to succeed trusts to no one but himself. When the rope was ready I made a parcel of my suit, my cloak, a few shirts, stockings, and handkerchiefs, and the three of us went into the count's cell. The first thing the count did was to congratulate Soradaci on having been placed in the same cell as myself, and on being so soon about to regain his liberty. His air of speechless confusion made me want to laugh. I took no more trouble about him, for I had thrown off the mask of Tartuffe which I had found terribly inconvenient all the time I had worn it for the rascal's sake. He knew, I could see, that he had been deceived, but he understood nothing else, as he could not make out how I could have arranged with the supposed angel to come and go at certain fixed times. He listened attentively to the count, who told us we were going to our destruction, and like the coward that he was, he began to plan how to escape from the dangerous journey. I told the monk to put his bundle together while I was making the hole in the roof by the side of the loft.

At eight o'clock, without needing any help, my opening was made. I had broken up the beams, and the space was twice the size required. I got the plate of lead off in one piece. I could not do it by myself, because it was riveted. The monk came to my aid, and by dint of driving the bar between the gutter and the lead I succeeded in loosening it, and then, heaving at it with our shoulders, we beat it up till the opening was wide enough. On putting my head out through the hole I was distressed to see the brilliant light of the crescent moon then entering in its first quarter. This was a piece of bad luck which must be borne patiently, and we should have to wait till midnight, when the moon would have gone to light up the Antipodes. On such a fine night as this everybody would be walking in St. Mark's Place, and I dared not shew myself on the roof as the moonlight would have thrown a huge shadow of me on the place, and have drawn towards me all eyes, especially those of Messer-Grande and his myrmidons, and our fine scheme would have been brought to nothing by their detestable activity. I immediately decided that we could not escape till after the moon set; in the mean time I prayed for the help of God, but did not ask Him to work any miracles for me. I was at the mercy of Fortune, and I had to take care not to give her any advantages; and if my scheme ended in failure I should be consoled by the thought that I had not made a single mistake. The moon would set at eleven and sunrise was at six, so we had seven hours of perfect darkness at our service; and though we had a hard task, I considered that in seven hours it would be accomplished.

I told Father Balbi that we could pass the three hours in talking to Count Asquin. I requested him to go first and ask the count to lend me thirty sequins, which would be as necessary to me as my pike had been hitherto. He carried my message, and a few minutes after came and asked me to go myself, as the count wished to talk to me alone. The poor old man began by saying with great politeness that I really stood in no need of money to escape, that he had none, that he had a large family, that if I was killed the money would be lost, with a thousand other futilities of the same kind to disguise his avarice, or the dislike he felt to parting with his money. My reply lasted for half an hour, and contained some excellent arguments, which never have had and never will have any force, as the finest weapons of oratory are blunted when used against one of the strongest of the passions. It was a matter of a 'nolenti baculus'; not that I was cruel enough to use force towards an unhappy old man like the count. I ended my speech by saying that if he would flee with us I would carry him upon my back like Æneas carried Anchises; but if he was going to stay in prison to offer up prayers for our success, his prayers would be observed, as it would be a case of praying

GIACOMO CASANOVA

God to give success when he himself had refused to contribute the most ordinary aid.

He replied by a flood of tears, which affected me. He then asked if two sequins would be enough, and I answered in the affirmative. He then gave them to me begging me to return them to him if after getting on the roof I saw my wisest course would be to come back. I promised to do so, feeling somewhat astonished that he should deem me capable of a retreat. He little knew me, for I would have preferred death to an imprisonment which would have been life-long.

I called my companions, and we set all our baggage near the hole. I divided the hundred fathoms of rope into two packets, and we spent two hours in talking over the chances of our undertaking. The first proof which Father Balbi gave me of his fine character was to tell me, ten times over, that I had broken my word with him, since I had assured him that my scheme was complete and certain, while it was really nothing of the kind. He went so far as to tell me that if he had known as much he would not have taken me from my cell. The count also, with all the weight of his seventy years, told me that I should do well to give up so hazardous an undertaking, in which success was impossible and death probable. As he was a barrister he made me a speech as follows, and I had not much difficulty in guessing that he was inspired by the thought of the two sequins which I should have had to give him back, if he had succeeded in persuading me to stay where I was:

"The incline of the roof covered with lead plates," said he, "will render it impossible for you to walk, indeed you will scarcely be able to stand on your feet. It is true that the roof has seven or eight windows, but they are all barred with iron, and you could not keep your footing near them since they are far from the sides. Your ropes are useless, as you will find nothing whereon to fasten them; and even if you did, a man descending from such a height cannot reach the ground by himself. One of you will therefore have to lower the two others one at a time as one lowers a bucket or a bundle of wood, and he who does so will have to stay behind and go back to his cell. Which of you three has a vocation for this dangerous work of charity? And supposing that one of you is heroic enough to do so, can you tell me on which side you are going to descend? Not by the side towards the palace, for you would be seen; not by the church, as you would find yourselves still shut up, and as to the court side you surely would not think of it, for you would fall into the hands of the 'arsenalotti' who are always going their rounds there. You have only the canal side left, and where is your gondola to take you off? Not having any such thing, you will be obliged to throw yourself in and escape by swimming towards St. Appollonia, which you will reach in a wretched condition, not knowing where to turn to next. You must remember that the leads are slippery, and that if you were to fall into the canal, considering the height of the fall and the shallowness of the water, you would most certainly be killed if you could swim like sharks. You would be crushed to death, for three or four feet of water are not sufficient to counteract the effect of a fall from such a height. In short, the best fate you can expect is to find yourselves on the ground with broken arms and legs."

The effect of this discourse—a very unseasonable one, under the circumstances—was to make my blood boil, but I listened with a patience wholly foreign to my nature. The rough reproaches of the monk enraged me, and inclined me to answer him in his own way; but I felt that my position was a difficult one, and that unless I was careful I might ruin all, for I had to do with a coward quite capable of saying that he was not going to risk his life, and by myself I could not hope to succeed. I constrained myself, therefore, and as politely as I could I told them that I was sure of success, though I could not as yet communicate the details of my plan. "I shall profit by your wise counsels," said I to Count Asquin, "and be very prudent, but my trust in God and in my own strength will carry me through all difficulties."

From time to time I stretched out my hand to assure myself that Soradaci was there, for he did not speak a word. I laughed to myself to think what he might be turning in his head now that he was convinced that I had deceived him. At half-past ten I told him to go and see what was the position of the moon. He obeyed and returned, saying that in an hour and a-half it would have disappeared, and that there was a thick fog which would make the leads very dangerous.

"All I ask," I said, "is that the fog be not made of oil. Put your cloak in a packet with some of the rope which must be divided equally between us."

At this I was astonished to find him at my knees kissing my hands, and entreating me not to kill him. "I should be sure," said he, "to fall over into the canal, and I should not be of any use to you. Ah! leave me here, and all the night I will pray to St. Francis for you. You can kill me or save me alive; but of this I am determined, never to follow you."

The fool never thought how he had responded to my prayers.

GIACOMO CASANOVA

"You are right," I said, "you may stop here on the condition that you will pray to St. Francis; and that you go forthwith and fetch my books, which I wish to leave to the count."

He did so without answering me, doubtless with much joy. My books were worth at least a hundred crowns. The count told me that he would give them back on my return.

"You may be sure," I said, "that you will never see me here again. The books will cover your expenditure of two sequins. As to this rascal, I am delighted, as he cannot muster sufficient courage to come with me. He would be in the way, and the fellow is not worthy of sharing with Father Balbi and myself the honours of so brave a flight."

"That's true," said the count, "provided that he does not congratulate himself to-morrow."

I asked the count to give me pens, ink, and paper, which he possessed in spite of the regulations to the contrary, for such prohibitions were nothing to Lawrence, who would have sold St. Mark himself for a crown. I then wrote the following letter, which I gave to Soradaci, not being able to read it over, as I had written it in the dark. I began by a fine heading, which I wrote in Latin, and which in English would run thus:

"'I shall not die, but live and declare the works of the Lord.'"

"Our lords of state are bound to do all in their power to keep a prisoner under the Leads, and on the other hand the prisoner, who is fortunately not on parole, is bound also to make his escape. Their right to act thus is founded on justice, while the prisoner follows the voice of nature; and since they have not asked him whether he will be put in prison, so he ought not to ask them leave to escape.

"Jacques Casanova, writing in the bitterness of his heart, knows that he may have the ill luck to be recaptured before he succeeds in leaving the Venetian territory and escaping to a friendly state; but if so, he appeals to the humanity of the judges not to add to the misery of the condition from which, yielding to the voice of nature, he is endeavouring to escape. He begs them, if he be taken, to return him whatever may be in his cell, but if he succeed he gives the whole to Francis Soradaci, who is still a captive for want of courage to escape, not like me preferring liberty to life. Casanova entreats their excellencies not to refuse the poor wretch this gift. Dated an hour before midnight, in the cell of Count Asquin, on October 31st, 1756."

I warned Soradaci not to give this letter to Lawrence, but to the secretary in person, who, no doubt, would interrogate him if he did not go himself to the cell, which was the more likely course. The count said my letter was perfect, but that he would give me back all my books if I returned. The fool said he wished to see me again to prove that he would return everything gladly.

But our time was come. The moon had set. I hung the half of the ropes by Father Balbi's neck on one side and his clothes on the other. I did the same to myself, and with our hats on and our coats off we went to the opening.

E quindi uscimmo a rimirar le stelle.—DANTE.

V

THE ESCAPE I NEARLY LOSE MY LIFE ON THE ROOF I GET
OUT OF THE DUCAL PALACE, TAKE A BOAT, AND REACH THE
MAINLAND—DANGER TO WHICH I AM EXPOSED BY FATHER
BALBI—MY SCHEME FOR RIDDING MYSELF OF HIM

I got out the first, and Father Balbi followed me. Soradaci who
had come as far as the opening, had orders to put the plate of
lead back in its place, and then to go and pray to St. Francis for
us. Keeping on my hands and knees, and grasping my pike firmly
I pushed it obliquely between the joining of the plates of lead, and
then holding the side of the plate which I had lifted I succeeded in
drawing myself up to the summit of the roof. The monk had taken
hold of my waistband to follow me, and thus I was like a beast of
burden who has to carry and draw along at the same time; and this
on a steep and slippery roof.

When we were half-way up the monk asked me to stop, as one of
his packets had slipped off, and he hoped it had not gone further than
the gutter. My first thought was to give him a kick and to send him
after his packet, but, praised be to God! I had sufficient self-control not
to yield to it, and indeed the punishment would have been too heavy
for both of us, as I should have had no chance of escaping by myself. I
asked him if it were the bundle of rope, and on his replying that it was
a small packet of his own containing manuscript he had found in one
of the garrets under the Leads, I told him he must bear it patiently, as
a single step might be our destruction. The poor monk gave a sigh, and
he still clinging to my waist we continued climbing.

After having surmounted with the greatest difficulty fifteen or
sixteen plates we got to the top, on which I sat astride, Father Balbi
imitating my example. Our backs were towards the little island of
St. George the Greater, and about two hundred paces in front of us
were the numerous cupolas of St. Mark's Church, which forms part of
the ducal palace, for St. Mark's is really the Doge's private chapel, and
no monarch in the world can boast of having a finer. My first step was
to take off my bundle, and I told my companion to do the same. He put
the rope as best he could upon his thighs, but wishing to take off his
hat, which was in his way, he took hold of it awkwardly, and it was soon

dancing from plate to plate to join the packet of linen in the gutter. My poor companion was in despair.

"A bad omen," he exclaimed; "our task is but begun and here am I deprived of shirt, hat, and a precious manuscript, containing a curious account of the festivals of the palace."

I felt calmer now that I was no longer crawling on hands and knees, and I told him quietly that the two accidents which had happened to him had nothing extraordinary in them, and that not even a superstitious person would call them omens, that I did not consider them in that light, and that they were far from damping my spirits.

"They ought rather," said I, "to warn you to be prudent, and to remind you that God is certainly watching over us, for if your hat had fallen to the left instead of to the right, we should have been undone; as in that case it would have fallen into the palace court, where it would have caught the attention of the guards, and have let them know that there was someone on the roof; and in a few minutes we should have been retaken."

After looking about me for some time I told the monk to stay still till I came back, and I set out, my pike in my hand, sitting astride the roof and moving along without any difficulty. For nearly an hour I went to this side and that, keeping a sharp look-out, but in vain; for I could see nothing to which the rope could be fastened, and I was in the greatest perplexity as to what was to be done. It was of no use thinking of getting down on the canal side or by the court of the palace, and the church offered only precipices which led to nothing. To get to the other side of the church towards the Canonica, I should have had to climb roofs so steep that I saw no prospect of success. The situation called for hardihood, but not the smallest piece of rashness.

It was necessary, however, either to escape, or to reenter the prison, perhaps never again to leave it, or to throw myself into the canal. In such a dilemma it was necessary to leave a good deal to chance, and to make a start of some kind. My eye caught a window on the canal sides, and two-thirds of the distance from the gutter to the summit of the roof. It was a good distance from the spot I had set out from, so I concluded that the garret lighted by it did not form part of the prison I had just broken. It could only light a loft, inhabited or uninhabited, above some rooms in the palace, the doors of which would probably be opened by day-break. I was morally sure that if the palace servants saw us they would help us to escape, and not deliver us over to the Inquisitors, even if they recognized us as criminals of the deepest dye; so heartily was the State Inquisition hated by everyone.

It was thus necessary for me to get in front of the window, and letting myself slide softly down in a straight line I soon found myself astride on top of the dormer-roof. Then grasping the sides I stretched my head over, and succeeded in seeing and touching a small grating, behind which was a window of square panes of glass joined with thin strips of lead. I did not trouble myself about the window, but the grating, small as it was, appeared an insurmountable difficulty, failing a file, and I had only my pike.

I was thoroughly perplexed, and was beginning to lose courage, when an incident of the simplest and most natural kind came to my aid and fortified my resolution.

Philosophic reader, if you will place yourself for a moment in my position, if you will share the sufferings which for fifteen months had been my lot, if you think of my danger on the top of a roof, where the slightest step in a wrong direction would have cost me my life, if you consider the few hours at my disposal to overcome difficulties which might spring up at any moment, the candid confession I am about to make will not lower me in your esteem; at any rate, if you do not forget that a man in an anxious and dangerous position is in reality only half himself.

It was the clock of St. Mark's striking midnight, which, by a violent shock, drew me out of the state of perplexity I had fallen into. The clock reminded me that the day just beginning was All Saints' Day—the day of my patron saint (at least if I had one)—and the prophecy of my confessor came into my mind. But I confess that what chiefly strengthened me, both bodily and mentally, was the profane oracle of my beloved Ariosto: 'Fra il fin d'ottobre, a il capo di novembre'.

The chime seemed to me a speaking talisman, commanding me to be up and doing,—and—promising me the victory. Lying on my belly I stretched my head down towards the grating, and pushing my pike into the sash which held it I resolved to take it out in a piece. In a quarter of an hour I succeeded, and held the whole grate in my hands,—and putting it on one side I easily broke the glass window, though wounding my left hand.

With the aid of my pike, using it as I had done before, I regained the ridge of the roof, and went back to the spot where I had left Balbi. I found him enraged and despairing, and he abused me heartily for having left him for so long. He assured me that he was only waiting for it to get light to return to the prison.

"What did you think had become of me?"

"I thought you must have fallen over."

"And you can find no better way than abuse to express the joy you ought to feel at seeing me again?"

"What have you been doing all this time?"

"Follow me, and you shall see."

I took up my packets again and made my way towards the window. As soon as were opposite to it I told Balbi what I had done, and asked him if he could think of any way of getting into the loft. For one it was easy enough, for the other could lower him by the rope; but I could not discover how the second of us was to get down afterwards, as there was nothing to which the rope could be fastened. If I let myself fall I might break my arms and legs, for I did not know the distance between the window and the floor of the room. To this chain of reasoning uttered in the friendliest possible tone, the brute replied thus:

"You let me down, and when I have got to the bottom you will have plenty of time to think how you are going to follow me."

I confess that my first indignant impulse was to drive my pike into his throat. My good genius stayed my arm, and I uttered not a word in reproach of his base selfishness. On the contrary, I straightway untied my bundle of rope and bound him strongly under the elbows, and making him lie flat down I lowered him feet foremost on to the roof of the dormer-window. When he got there I told him to lower himself into the window as far as his hips, supporting himself by holding his elbows against the sides of the window. As soon as he had done so, I slid down the roof as before, and lying down on the dormer-roof with a firm grasp of the rope I told the monk not to be afraid but to let himself go. When he reached the floor of the loft he untied himself, and on drawing the rope back I found the fall was one of fifty feet-too dangerous a jump to be risked. The monk who for two hours had been a prey to terror; seated in a position which I confess was not a very reassuring one, was not quite cool, and called out to me to throw him the ropes for him to take care of—a piece of advice you may be sure I took care not to follow.

Not knowing what to do next, and waiting for some fortunate idea, I made my way back to the ridge of the roof, and from there spied out a corner near a cupola; which I had not visited. I went towards it and found a flat roof, with a large window closed with two shutters. At hand was a tubful of plaster, a trowel, and ladder which I thought long enough for my purpose. This was enough, and tying my rope to the first round I dragged this troublesome burden after me to the window. My next task was to get the end of the ladder (which was twelve fathoms long) into the opening, and the difficulties I encountered made me sorry that I had deprived myself of the aid of the monk. (The unit of measure: 'fathoms' describing the ladder and earlier the 100 fathoms of rope, is likely a translation error: Casanova might have manufactured 100 feet of rope and might have dragged a 12 foot ladder up the steep roof, but not a longer. D.W.)

I had set the ladder in such a way that one end touched the window, and the other went below the gutter. I next slid down to the roof of the window, and drawing the ladder towards me I fastened the end of my rope to the eighth round, and then let it go again till it was parallel with the window. I then strove to get it in, but I could not insert it farther than the fifth round, for the end of the ladder being stopped by the inside roof of the window no force on earth could have pushed it any further without breaking either the ladder or the ceiling. There was nothing to be done but to lift it by the other end; it would then slip down by its own weight. I might, it is true, have placed the ladder across the window, and have fastened the rope to it, in which manner I might have let myself down into the loft without any risk; but the ladder would have been left outside to shew Lawrence and the guards where to look for us and possibly to find us in the morning.

I did not care to risk by a piece of imprudence the fruit of so much toil and danger, and to destroy all traces of our whereabouts the ladder must be drawn in. Having no one to give me a helping hand, I resolved to go myself to the parapet to lift the ladder and attain the end I had in view. I did so, but at such a hazard as had almost cost me my life. I could let go the ladder while I slackened the rope without any fear of its falling over, as it had caught to the parapet by the third rung. Then, my pike in my hand, I slid down beside the ladder to the parapet, which held up the points of my feet, as I was lying on my belly. In this position I pushed the ladder forward, and was able to get it into the window to the length of a foot, and that diminished by a good deal its weight. I now only had to push it in another two feet, as I was sure that I could get it in altogether by means of the rope from the roof of the window. To impel the ladder to the extent required I got on my knees, but the effort I had to use made me slip, and in an instant I was over the parapet as far as my chest, sustained by my elbows.

I shudder still when I think of this awful moment, which cannot be conceived in all its horror. My natural instinct made me almost unconsciously strain every nerve to regain the parapet, and—I had nearly said miraculously—I succeeded. Taking care not to let myself slip back an inch I struggled upwards with my hands and arms, while my belly was resting on the edge of the parapet. Fortunately the ladder was safe, for with that unlucky effort which had nearly cost me so dearly I had pushed it in more than three feet, and there it remained.

Finding myself resting on my groin on the parapet, I saw that I had only to lift up my right leg and to put up first one knee and then the other to be absolutely out of danger; but I had not yet got to the end of my trouble. The effort I made gave me so severe a spasm that I became cramped and unable to use my limbs. However, I did not lose my head, but kept quiet till the pain had gone off, knowing by experience that keeping still is the best cure for the false cramp. It was a dreadful moment! In two minutes I made another effort, and had the good fortune to get my two knees on to the parapet, and as soon as I had taken breath I cautiously hoisted the ladder and pushed it half-way through the window. I then took my pike, and crawling up as I had done before I reached the window, where my knowledge of the laws of equilibrium and leverage aided me to insert the ladder to its full length, my companion receiving the end of it. I then threw into the loft the bundles and the fragments that I had broken off the window, and I stepped down to the monk, who welcomed me heartily and drew in the ladder. Arm in arm, we proceeded to inspect the gloomy retreat in which we found ourselves, and judged it to be about thirty paces long by twenty wide.

At one end were folding-doors barred with iron. This looked bad, but putting my hand to the latch in the middle it yielded to the pressure, and the door opened. The first thing we did was to make the tour of the room, and crossing it we stumbled against a large table surrounded by stools and armchairs. Returning to the part where we had seen windows, we opened the shutters of one of them, and the light of the stars only shewed us: the cupolas and the depths beneath them. I did not think for a moment of lowering myself down, as I wished to know where I was going, and I did not recognize our surroundings. I shut the window up, and we returned to the place where we had left our packages. Quite exhausted I let myself fall on the floor, and placing a bundle of rope under my head a sweet sleep came to my relief. I abandoned myself to it without resistance, and indeed, I believe if death were to have been the result, I should have slept all the same, and I still remember how I enjoyed that sleep.

It lasted for three and a half hours, and I was awakened by the monk's calling out and shaking me. He told me that it had just struck five. He said it was inconceivable to him how I could sleep in the situation we were in. But that which was inconceivable to him was not so to me. I had not fallen asleep on purpose, but had only yielded to the demands of exhausted nature, and, if I may say so, to the extremity of my need. In my exhaustion there was nothing to wonder at, since I had neither eaten nor slept for two days, and the efforts I had made—efforts almost beyond the limits of mortal endurance—might well have exhausted any man. In my sleep my activity had come back to me, and I was delighted to see the darkness disappearing, so that we should be able to proceed with more certainty and quickness.

Casting a rapid glance around, I said to myself, "This is not a prison, there ought, therefore, be some easy exit from it." We addressed ourselves to the end opposite to the folding-doors, and in a narrow recess I thought I made out a doorway. I felt it over and touched a lock, into which I thrust my pike, and opened it with three or four heaves. We then found ourselves in a small room, and I discovered a key on a table, which I tried on a door opposite to us, which, however, proved to be unlocked. I told the monk to go for our bundles, and replacing the key we passed out and came into a gallery containing presses full of papers. They were the state archives. I came across a short flight of stone stairs, which I descended, then another, which I descended also, and found a glass door at the end, on opening which I entered a hall well known to me: we were in the ducal chancery. I opened a window and could have got down easily, but the result would have been that we should have been trapped in the maze of little courts around St. Mark's Church. I saw on a desk an iron instrument, of which I took possession; it had a rounded point and a wooden handle, being used by the clerks of the chancery to pierce parchments for the purpose of affixing the leaden seals. On opening the desk I saw the copy of a letter advising the Proveditore of Corfu of a grant of three thousand sequins for the restoration of the old fortress. I searched for the sequins but they were not there. God knows how gladly I would have taken them, and how I would have laughed the monk to scorn if he had accused me of theft! I should have received the money as a gift from Heaven, and should have regarded myself as its master by conquest.

Going to the door of the chancery, I put my bar in the keyhole, but finding immediately that I could not break it open, I resolved on making a hole in the door. I took care to choose the side where the wood had fewest knots, and working with all speed I struck as hard and as cleaving strokes as I was able. The monk, who helped me as well as he could with the punch I had taken from the desk, trembled at the echoing clamour of my pike which must have been audible at some distance. I felt the danger myself, but it had to be risked.

In half an hour the hole was large enough—a fortunate circumstance, for I should have had much trouble in making it any larger without the aid of a saw. I was afraid when I looked at the edges of the hole, for they bristled with jagged pieces of wood which seemed made for tearing clothes and flesh together. The hole was at a height of five feet from the ground. We placed beneath it two stools, one beside the other, and when we had stepped upon them the monk with arms crossed and head foremost began to make his way through the hole, and taking him by the thighs, and afterwards by the legs, I succeeded in pushing him through, and though it was dark I felt quite secure, as I knew the surroundings. As soon as my companion had reached the other side I threw him my belongings, with the exception of the ropes, which I left behind, and placing a third stool on the two others, I climbed up, and got through as far as my middle, though with much difficulty, owing to the extreme narrowness of the hole. Then, having nothing to grasp with my hands, nor anyone to push me as I had pushed the monk, I asked him to take me, and draw me gently and by slow degrees towards him. He did so, and I endured silently the fearful torture I had to undergo, as my thighs and legs were torn by the splinters of wood.

As soon as I got through I made haste to pick up my bundle of linen, and going down two flights of stairs I opened without difficulty the door leading into the passage whence opens the chief door to the grand staircase, and in another the door of the closet of the 'Savio alla scrittura'. The chief door was locked, and I saw at once that, failing a catapult or a mine of gunpowder, I could not possibly get through. The bar I still held seemed to say, "Hic fines posuit. My use is ended and you can lay me down." It was dear to me as the instrument of freedom, and was worthy of being hung as an 'ex voto' on the altar of liberty.

I sat down with the utmost tranquillity, and told the monk to do the same.

"My work is done," I said, "the rest must be left to God and fortune.

"Abbia chi regge il ciel cura del resto, O la fortuna se non tocca a lui.

"I do not know whether those who sweep out the palace will come here to-day, which is All Saints' Day, or tomorrow, All Souls' Day. If anyone comes, I shall run out as soon as the door opens, and do you follow after me; but if nobody comes, I do not budge a step, and if I die of hunger so much the worse for me."

At this speech of mine he became beside himself. He called me a madman, seducer, deceiver, and a liar. I let him talk, and took no notice. It struck six; only an hour had passed since I had my awakening in the loft.

My first task was to change my clothes. Father Balbi looked like a peasant, but he was in better condition than I, his clothes were not torn to shreds or covered with blood, his red flannel waistcoat and purple breeches were intact, while my figure could only inspire pity or terror, so bloodstained and tattered was I. I took off my stockings, and the blood gushed out of two wounds I had given myself on the parapet, while the splinters in the hole in the door had torn my waistcoat, shirt, breeches, legs and thighs. I was dreadfully wounded all over my body. I made bandages of handkerchiefs, and dressed my wounds as best I could, and then put on my fine suit, which on a winter's day would look odd enough. Having tied up my hair, I put on white stockings, a laced shirt, failing any other, and two others over it, and then stowing away some stockings and handkerchiefs in my pockets, I threw everything else into a corner of the room. I flung my fine cloak over the monk, and the fellow looked as if he had stolen it. I must have looked like a man who has been to a dance and has spent the rest of the night in a disorderly house, though the only foil to my reasonable elegance of attire was the bandages round my knees.

In this guise, with my exquisite hat trimmed with Spanish lace and adorned with a white feather on my head, I opened a window. I was immediately remarked by some lounger in the palace court, who, not understanding what anyone of my appearance was doing there at such an early hour, went to tell the door-keeper of the circumstance. He, thinking he must have locked somebody in the night before, went for his keys and came towards us. I was sorry to have let myself be seen at the window, not knowing that therein chance was working for our escape, and was sitting down listening to the idle talk of the monk, when I heard the jingling of keys. Much perturbed I got up and put my eye to a chink in the door, and saw a man with a great bunch of keys in his hand mounting leisurely up the stairs. I told the monk not to open his mouth, to keep well behind me, and to follow my steps. I took my pike, and concealing it in my right sleeve I got into a corner by the door, whence I could get out as soon as it was opened and run down the stairs. I prayed that the man might make no resistance, as if he did I should be obliged to fell him to the earth, and I determined to do so.

The door opened; and the poor man as soon as he saw me seemed turned to a stone. Without an instant's delay and in dead silence, I made haste to descend the stairs, the monk following me. Avoiding the appearance of a fugitive, but walking fast, I went by the giants' Stairs, taking no notice of Father Balbi, who kept cabling: out "To the church! to the church!"

The church door was only about twenty paces from the stairs, but the churches were no longer sanctuaries in Venice; and no one ever took refuge in them. The monk knew this, but fright had deprived him of his faculties. He told me afterwards that the motive which impelled him to go to the church was the voice of religion bidding him seek the horns of the altar.

"Why didn't you go by yourself?" said I.

"I did not, like to abandon you," but he should rather have said, "I did not like to lose the comfort of your company."

The safety I sought was beyond the borders of the Republic, and thitherward I began to bend my steps. Already there in spirit, I must needs be there in body also. I went straight towards the chief door of the palace, and looking at no one that might be tempted to look at me I got to the canal and entered the first gondola that I came across, shouting to the boatman on the poop,

"I want to go to Fusina; be quick and, call another gondolier."

This was soon done, and while the gondola was being got off I sat down on the seat in the middle, and Balbi at the side. The odd appearance of the monk, without a hat and with a fine cloak on his shoulders, with my unseasonable attire, was enough to make people take us for an astrologer and his man.

As soon as we had passed the custom-house, the gondoliers began to row with a will along the Giudecca Canal, by which we must pass to go to Fusina or to Mestre, which latter place was really our destination. When we had traversed half the length of the canal I put my head out, and said to the waterman on the poop,

"When do you think we shall get to Mestre?"

"But you told me to go to Fusina."

"You must be mad; I said Mestre."

The other boatman said that I was mistaken, and the fool of a monk, in his capacity of zealous Christian and friend of truth, took care to tell me that I was wrong. I wanted to give him a hearty kick as a punishment for his stupidity, but reflecting that common sense comes not by wishing for it I burst into a peal of laughter, and agreed that I might have made a mistake, but that my real intention was to go to Mestre. To that they answered nothing, but a minute after the master boatman said he was ready to take me to England if I liked.

"Bravely spoken," said I, "and now for Mestre, ho!"

"We shall be there in three quarters of an hour, as the wind and tide are in our favour."

Well pleased I looked at the canal behind us, and thought it had never seemed so fair, especially as there was not a single boat coming our way. It was a glorious morning, the air was clear and glowing with the first rays of the sun, and my two young watermen rowed easily and well; and as I thought over the night of sorrow, the dangers I had escaped, the abode where I had been fast bound the day before, all the chances which had been in my favour, and the liberty of which I now began to taste the sweets, I was so moved in my heart and grateful to my God that, well nigh choked with emotion, I burst into tears.

My nice companion who had hitherto only spoken to back up the gondoliers, thought himself bound to offer me his consolations. He did not understand why I was weeping, and the tone he took made me pass from sweet affliction to a strange mirthfulness which made him go astray once more, as he thought I had got mad. The poor monk, as I have said, was a fool, and whatever was bad about him was the result of his folly. I had been under the sad necessity of turning him to account, but though without intending to do so he had almost been my ruin. It was no use trying to make him believe that I had told the gondoliers to go to Fusina whilst I intended to go to Mestre; he said I could not have thought of that till I got on to the Grand Canal.

In due course we reached Mestre. There were no horses to ride post, but I found men with coaches who did as well, and I agreed with one of them to take me to Trevisa in an hour and a quarter. The horses were put in in three minutes, and with the idea that Father Balbi was behind me I turned round to say "Get up," but he was not there. I told an ostler to go and look for him, with the intention of reprimanding him sharply, even if he had gone for a necessary occasion, for we had no time to waste, not even thus. The man came back saying he could not find' him, to my great rage and indignation. I was tempted to abandon him, but a feeling of humanity restrained me. I made enquiries all round; everybody had seen him, but not a soul knew where he was. I walked along the High Street, and some instinct prompting me to put my head in at the window of a cafe. I saw the wretched man standing at the bar drinking chocolate and making love to the girl. Catching sight of me, he pointed to the girl and said—

"She's charming," and then invited me to take a cup of chocolate, saying that I must pay, as he hadn't a penny. I kept back my wrath and answered,

"I don't want any, and do you make haste!" and caught hold of his arm in such sort that he turned white with pain. I paid the money and we went out. I trembled with anger. We got into our coach, but we had scarcely gone ten paces before I recognised: an inhabitant, of Mestre named Balbi Tommasi, a good sort of man; but reported to be one of the familiars of the Holy Office. He knew me, too, and coming up called out,

"I am delighted to see you here. I suppose you have just escaped. How did you do it?"

"I have not escaped, but have been set at liberty."

"No, no, that's not possible, as I was at M. Grimani's yesterday evening, and I should have heard of it."

It will be easier for the reader to imagine my state of mind than for me to describe it. I was discovered by a man whom I believed to be a hired agent of the Government, who only had to give a glance to one of the sbirri with whom Mestre swarmed to have me arrested. I told him to speak softly, and getting down I asked him to come to one side. I took him behind a house, and seeing that there was nobody in sight, a ditch in front, beyond which the open country extended, I grasped my pike and took him by the neck. At this: he gave a struggle, slipped out of my hands, leapt over the ditch, and without turning round set off to run at, full speed. As soon as he was some way off he slackened his course, turned round and kissed his hand to me, in token of wishing me a prosperous journey. And as soon; as he was out of my sight I gave thanks to God that, this man by his quickness had preserved me from the commission of a crime, for I would have killed him; and he, as it turned out, bore me no ill will.

I was in a terrible position. In open war with all the powers of-the Republic, everything had to give way to my safety, which made me neglect no means of attaining my ends.

With the gloom of a man who has passed through a great peril, I gave a glance of contempt towards the monk, who now saw to what danger he had exposed us, and then got up again into the carriage. We reached Trevisa without further adventure, and I told the posting-master to get me a carriage and two horses ready by ten o'clock; though I had no intention of continuing my journey along the highway, both because I lacked means; and because I feared pursuit. The inn-keeper asked me, if I would take any breakfast, of which I stood in great need, for I was dying with hunger, but I did not dare to, accept his offer, as a quarter of an hour's delay might, prove fatal. I was afraid of being retaken, and of being ashamed of it for the rest of my life; for a man of sense ought to be able to snap his fingers at four hundred thousand men in the open country, and if he cannot escape capture he must be a fool.

I went out by St. Thomas's Gate as if I was going for a short walk, and after walking for a mile on the highway I struck into the fields, resolving not to leave them as long as I should be within the borders of the Republic. The shortest way was by Bassano, but I took the longer path, thinking I might possibly be expected on the more direct road, while they would never think of my leaving the Venetian territory by way of Feltre, which is the longest way of getting into the state subject to the Bishop of Trent.

After walking for three hours I let myself drop to the ground, for I could not move a step further. I must either take some food or die there, so I told the monk to leave the cloak with me and go to a farm I saw, there to buy something to eat. I gave him the money, and he set off, telling me that he thought I had more courage. The miserable man did not know what courage was, but he was more robust than myself, and he had, doubtless, taken in provisions before leaving the prison. Besides he had had some chocolate; he was thin and wiry, and a monk, and mental anxieties were unknown to him.

Although the house was not an inn, the good farmer's wife sent me a sufficient meal which only cost me thirty Venetian sous. After satisfying my appetite, feeling that sleep was creeping on me, I set out again on the tramp, well braced up. In four hours' time I stopped at a hamlet, and found that I was twenty-four miles from Trevisa. I was done up, my ankles were swollen, and my shoes were in holes. There was only another hour of day-light before us. Stretching myself out beneath a grove of trees I made Father Balbi sit by me, and discoursed to him in the manner following:

"We must make for Borgo di Valsugano, it is the first town beyond the borders of the Republic. We shall be as safe there as if we were in London, and we can take our ease for awhile; but to get there we must go carefully to work, and the first thing we must do is to separate. You must go by Mantello Woods, and I by the mountains; you by the easiest and shortest way, and I by the longest and most difficult; you with money and I without a penny. I will make you a present of my cloak, which you must exchange for a great coat and a hat, and everybody will take you for a countryman, as you are luckily rather like one in the face. Take these seventeen livres, which is all that remains to me of the two sequins Count Asquin gave me. You will reach Borgo by the day after to-morrow, and I shall be twenty-four hours later. Wait for me in the first inn on the left-hand side of the street, and be sure I shall come in due season. I require a good night's rest in a good bed; and Providence will get me one somewhere, but I must sleep without fear of being disturbed, and in your company that would be out of the question. I am certain that we are being sought for on all sides, and that our descriptions have been so correctly given that if we went into any inn together we should be certain to be arrested. You see the state I am in, and my urgent necessity for a ten hours' rest. Farewell, then, do you go that way and I will take this, and I will find somewhere near here a rest for the sole of my foot."

"I have been expecting you to say as much," said Father Balbi, "and for answer I will remind you of the promise you gave me when I let myself be persuaded to break into your cell. You promised me that we should always keep company; and so don't flatter yourself that I shall leave you, your fate and mine are linked together. We shall be able to get a good refuge for our money, we won't go to the inns, and no one will arrest us."

"You are determined, are you, not to follow the good advice I have given you?"

"I am."

"We shall see about that."

I rose to my feet, though with some difficulty, and taking the measure of his height I marked it out upon the ground, then drawing my pike from my pocket, I proceeded with the utmost coolness to excavate the earth, taking no notice of the questions the monk asked me. After working: for a quarter of an hour I set myself to gaze sadly upon him, and I told him that I felt obliged as a Christian to warn him to commend his soul to God, "since I am about to bury you here, alive or dead; and if you prove the stronger, you will bury me. You can escape if you wish to, as I shall not pursue you."

He made no reply, and I betook myself to my work again, but I confess that I began to be afraid of being rushed to extremities by this brute, of whom I was determined to rid myself.

At last, whether convinced by my arguments or afraid Of my pike, he came towards me. Not guessing. What he was about, I presented the point of my pike towards him, but I had nothing to fear.

"I will do what you want," said he.

I straightway gave him all the money I had, and promising to rejoin him at Borgo I bade him farewell. Although I had not a penny in my pocket and had two rivers to cross over, I congratulated myself on having got rid of a man of his character, for by myself I felt confident of being able to cross the bounds of the Republic.

VI

I Find a Lodging in the House of the Chief of the Sbirri—
I Pass a Good Night There and Recover My Strength—
I Go to Mass—A Disagreeable Meeting I am Obliged to
Take Six Sequins by Force—Out of Danger—Arrived
at Munich—Balbi I Set Out for Paris—My Arrival—
Attempt on the Life of Louis XV

As soon as I saw Father Balbi far enough off I got up, and seeing at a little distance a shepherd keeping his flock on the hill-side, I made my way-towards him to obtain such information as I needed. "What is the name of this village, my friend?" said I.

"Valde Piadene, signor," he answered, to my surprise, for I found I was much farther on my way that I thought. I next asked him the owners of five or six houses which I saw scattered around, and the persons he mentioned chanced to be all known to me, but were not the kind of men I should have cared to trouble with my presence. On my asking him the name of a palace before me, he said it belonged to the Grimanis, the chief of whom was a State Inquisitor, and then resident at the palace, so I had to take care not to let him see me. Finally, an my enquiring the owner of a red house in the distance, he told me, much to my surprise, that it belonged to the chief of the sbirri. Bidding farewell to the kindly shepherd I began to go down the hill mechanically, and I am still puzzled to know what instinct directed my steps towards that house, which common sense and fear also should have made me shun. I steered my course for it in a straight line, and I can say with truth that I did so quite unwittingly. If it be true that we have all of us an invisible intelligence—a beneficent genius who guides our steps aright—as was the case with Socrates, to that alone I should attribute the irresistible attraction which drew me towards the house where I had most to dread. However that may be, it was the boldest stroke I have played in my whole life.

I entered with an easy and unconstrained air, and asked a child who was playing at top in the court-yard where his father was. Instead of replying, the child went to call his mother, and directly afterwards appeared a pretty woman in the family way, who politely asked me my business with her husband, apologizing for his absence.

"I am sorry," I said, "to hear that my gossip is not in, though at the same time I am delighted to make the acquaintance of his charming wife."

"Your gossip? You will be M. Vetturi, then? My husband told me that you had kindly promised to be the god-father of our next child. I am delighted to know you, but my husband will be very vexed to have been away:

"I hope he will soon return, as I wanted to ask him for a night's lodging. I dare not go anywhere in the state you see me."

"You shall have the best bed in the house, and I will get you a good supper. My husband when he comes back will thank your excellence for doing us so much honour. He went away with all his people an hour ago, and I don't expect him back for three or four days."

"Why is he away for such a long time, my dear madam?"

"You have not heard, then, that two prisoners have escaped from The Leads? One is a noble and the other a private individual named Casanova. My husband has received a letter from Messer-Grande ordering him to make a search for them; if he find them he will take them back to Venice, and if not he will return here, but he will be on the look-out for three days at least."

"I am sorry for this accident, my dear madam, but I should not like to put you out, and indeed I should be glad to lie down immediately."

"You shall do so, and my mother shall attend to your wants. But what is the matter with your knees?"

"I fell down whilst hunting on the mountains, and gave myself some severe wounds, and am much weakened by loss of blood."

"Oh! my poor gentleman, my poor gentleman! But my mother will cure you."

She called her mother, and having told her of my necessities she went out. This pretty sbirress had not the wit of her profession, for the story I had told her sounded like a fairy-tale. On horseback with white silk stockings! Hunting in sarcenet, without cloak and without a man! Her husband would make fine game of her when he came back; but God bless her for her kind heart and benevolent stupidity. Her mother tended me with all the politeness I should have met with in the best families. The worthy woman treated me like a mother, and called me "son" as she attended to my wounds. The name sounded pleasantly in my ears, and did no little towards my cure by the sentiments it awoke in my breast. If I had been less taken up with the position I was in I should have repaid her care with some evident marks of the gratitude I felt, but the place I was in and the part I was playing made the situation too serious a one for me to think of anything else.

This kindly woman, after looking at my knees and my thighs, told me that I must make my mind to suffer a little pain, but I might be sure of being cured by the morning. All I had to do was to bear the application of medicated linen to my wounds, and not to stir till the next day. I promised to bear the pain patiently, and to do exactly as she told me.

I was given an excellent supper, and I ate and drank with good appetite. I then gave myself up to treatment, and fell asleep whilst my nurse was attending to me. I suppose she undressed me as she would a child, but I remembered nothing about it when I woke up—I was, in fact, totally unconscious. Though I had made a good supper I had only done so to satisfy my craving for food and to regain my strength, and sleep came to me with an irresistible force, as my physical exhaustion did not leave me the power of arguing myself out of it. I took my supper at six o'clock in the evening, and I heard six striking as I awoke. I seemed to have been enchanted. Rousing myself up and gathering my wits together, I first took off the linen bandages, and I was astonished to find my wounds healed and quite free from pain. I did my hair, dressed myself in less than five minutes, and finding the door of my room open I went downstairs, crossed the court, and left the house behind me, without appearing to notice two individuals who were standing outside, and must have been sbirri. I made haste to lengthen the distance between me and the place where I had found the kindliest hospitality, the utmost politeness, the most tender care, and best of all, new health and strength, and as I walked I could not help feeling terrified at the danger I had been in. I shuddered involuntarily; and at the present moment, after so many years, I still shudder when I think of the peril to which I had so heedlessly exposed myself. I wondered how I managed to go in, and still more how I came out; it seemed absurd that I should not be followed. For five hours I tramped on, keeping to the woods and mountains, not meeting a soul besides a few countryfolk, and turning neither to the right nor left.

It was not yet noon, when, as I went along my way, I stopped short at the sound of a bell. I was on high ground, and looking in the direction from which the sound came I saw, a little church in the valley, and many, people going towards it to hear mass. My heart desired to express thankfulness for the protection of Providence, and, though all nature was a temple worthy of its Creator, custom drew me to the church. When men are in trouble, every passing thought seems an inspiration. It was All Souls' Day. I went down the hill, and came into the church, and saw, to my astonishment, M. Marc Antoine Grimani, the nephew of the State Inquisitor, with Madame Marie Visani, his wife. I made my bow; which was returned, and after I had heard mass I left the church. M. Grimani followed me by himself, and when he had got near me, called me by name, saying, "What are you doing here, Casanova, and what has become of your friend?"

"I have given him what little money I had for him to escape by another road, whilst I, without a penny in my pocket, am endeavouring to reach a place of safety by this way. If your excellence would kindly give me some help, it would speed my journey for me."

"I can't give you anything, but you will find recluses on your way who won't let you die of hunger. But tell me how you contrived to pierce the roof of The Leads."

"The story is an interesting one, but it would take up too much time, and in the meanwhile the recluses might eat up the food which is to keep me from dying of hunger."

With this sarcasm I made him a profound bow, and went upon my way. In spite of my great want, his refusal pleased me, as it made me think myself a better gentleman than the "excellence" who had referred me to the charity of recluses. I heard at Paris afterwards that when his wife heard of it she reproached him for his hard-hearted behaviour. There can be no doubt that kindly and generous feelings are more often to be found in the hearts of women than of men.

I continued my journey till sunset. Weary and faint with hunger I stopped at a good-looking house, which stood by itself. I asked to speak to the master, and the porter told me that he was not in as he had gone to a wedding on the other side of the river, and would be away for two days, but that he had bidden him to welcome all his friends while he was away. Providence! luck! chance! whichever you like.

I went in and was treated to a good supper and a good bed. I found by the addresses of some letters which were lying about that I was being entertained in the house of M. Rombenchi—a consul, of what nation I know not. I wrote a letter to him and sealed it to await his return. After making an excellent supper and having had a good sleep, I rose, and dressing myself carefully set out again without being able to leave the porter any mark of my gratitude, and shortly afterwards crossed the river, promising to pay when I came back. After walking for five hours I dined in a monastery of Capuchins, who are very useful to people in my position. I then set out again, feeling fresh and strong, and walked along at a good pace till three o'clock. I halted at a house which I found from a countryman belonged to a friend of mine. I walked in, asked if the master was at home, and was shewn into a room where he was writing by himself. I stepped forward to greet him, but as soon as he saw me he seemed horrified and bid me be gone forthwith, giving me idle and insulting reasons for his behaviour. I explained to him how I was situated, and asked him to let me have sixty sequins on my note of hand, drawn on M. de Bragadin. He replied that he could not so much as give me a glass of water, since he dreaded the wrath of the Tribunal for my very presence in his house. He was a stockbroker, about sixty years old, and was under great obligations to me. His inhuman refusal produced quite a different effect on me than that of M. Grimani. Whether from rage, indignation, or nature, I took him by the collar, I shewed him my pike, and raising my voice threatened to kill him. Trembling all over, he took a key from his pocket and shewing me a bureau told me he kept money there, and I had only to open it and take what I wanted; I told him to open it himself. He did so, and on his opening a drawer containing gold, I told him to count me out six sequins.

"You asked me for sixty."

"Yes, that was when I was asking a loan of you as a friend; but since I owe the money to force, I require six only, and I will give you no note of hand. You shall be repaid at Venice, where I shall write of the pass to which you forced me, you cowardly wretch!"

"I beg your pardon! take the sixty sequins, I entreat you."

"No, no more. I am going on my way, and I advise you not to hinder me, lest in my despair I come back and burn your house about your ears."

I went out and walked for two hours, until the approach of night and weariness made me stop short at the house of a farmer, where I had a bad supper and a bed of straw. In the morning, I bought an old overcoat, and hired an ass to journey on, and near Feltre I bought a pair of boots. In this guise I passed the hut called the Scala. There was a guard there who, much to my delight, as the reader will guess, did not even honour me by asking my name. I then took a two-horse carriage and got to Borgo de Valsugano in good time, and found Father Balbi at the inn I had told him of. If he had not greeted me first I should not have known him. A great overcoat, a low hat over a thick cotton cap, disguised him to admiration. He told me that a farmer had given him these articles in exchange for my cloak, that he had arrived without difficulty, and was faring well. He was kind enough to tell me that he did not expect to see me, as he did not believe my promise to rejoin him was made in good faith. Possibly I should have been wise not to undeceive him on this account.

I passed the following day in the inn, where, without getting out of my bed, I wrote more than twenty letters to Venice, in many of which I explained what I had been obliged to do to get the six sequins.

The monk wrote impudent letters to his superior, Father Barbarigo, and to his brother nobles, and love-letters to the servant girls who had been his ruin. I took the lace off my dress, and sold my hat, and thus got rid of a gay appearance unsuitable to my position, as it made me too much an object of notice.

The next day I went to Pergina and lay there, and was visited by a young Count d'Alberg, who had discovered, in some way or another, that we had escaped from the state-prisons of Venice. From Pergina I went to Trent and from there to Bolzan, where, needing money for my dress, linen, and the continuation of my journey, I introduced myself to an old banker named Mensch, who gave me a man to send to Venice with a letter to M. de Bragadin. In the mean time the old banker put me in a good inn where I spent the six days the messenger was away in bed. He brought me the sum of a hundred sequins, and my first care was to clothe my companion, and afterwards myself. Every day I found the society of the wretched Balbi more intolerable. "Without me you would never have escaped" was continually in his mouth, and he kept reminding me that I had promised him half of whatever money I got. He made love to all the servant girls, and as he had neither the figure nor the manners to please them, his attentions were returned with good hearty slaps, which he bore patiently, but was as outrageous as ever in the course of twenty-four hours. I was amused, but at the same time vexed to be coupled to a man of so low a nature.

We travelled post, and in three days we got to Munich, where I went to lodge at the sign of the "Stag." There I found two young Venetians of the Cantarini family, who had been there some time in company with Count Pompei, a Veronese; but not knowing them, and having no longer any need of depending on recluses for my daily bread, I did not care to pay my respects to them. It was otherwise with Countess Coronini, whom I knew at St. Justine's Convent at Venice, and who stood very well with the Bavarian Court.

This illustrious lady, then seventy years old, gave me a good reception and promised to speak on my behalf to the Elector, with a view to his granting me an asylum in his country. The next day, having fulfilled her promise, she told me that his highness had nothing to say against me, but as for Balbi there was no safety for him in Bavaria, for as a fugitive monk he might be claimed by the monks at Munich, and his highness had no wish to meddle with the monks. The countess advised me therefore to get him out of the town as soon as possible, for him to fly to some other quarter, and thus to avoid the bad turn which his beloved brethren the monks were certain to do him.

Feeling in duty bound to look after the interests of the wretched fellow, I went to the Elector's confessor to ask him to give Balbi letters of introduction to some town in Swabia. The confessor, a Jesuit, did not give the lie to the fine reputation of his brethren of the order; his reception of me was as discourteous as it well could be. He told me in a careless way that at Munich I was well known. I asked him without flinching if I was to take this as a piece of good or bad news; but he made no answer, and left me standing. Another priest told me that he had gone out to verify the truth of a miracle of which the whole town was talking.

"What miracle is that, reverend father?" I said.

"The empress, the widow of Charles VII, whose body is still exposed to the public gaze, has warm feet, although she is dead."

"Perhaps something keeps them warm."

"You can assure yourself personally of the truth of this wonderful circumstance."

To neglect such an opportunity would have been to lose the chance of mirth or edification, and I was as desirous of the one as of the other. Wishing to be able to boast that I had seen a miracle—and one, moreover, of a peculiar interest for myself, who have always had the misfortune to suffer from cold feet—I went to see the mighty dead. It was quite true that her feet were warm, but the matter was capable of a simple explanation, as the feet of her defunct majesty were turned towards a burning lamp at a little distance off. A dancer of my acquaintance, whom curiosity had brought there with the rest, came up to me, complimented me upon my fortunate escape, and told me everybody was talking about it. His news pleased me, as it is always a good thing to interest the public. This son of Terpsichore asked me to dinner, and I was glad to accept his invitation. His name was Michel de l'Agata, and his wife was the pretty Gandela, whom I had known sixteen years ago at the old Malipiero's. The Gandela was enchanted to see me, and to hear from my own lips the story of my wondrous escape. She interested herself on behalf of the monk, and offered me to give him a letter of introduction for Augsburg Canon Bassi, of Bologna, who was Dean of St. Maurice's Chapter, and a friend of hers. I took advantage of the offer, and she forthwith wrote me the letter, telling me that I need not trouble myself any more about the monk, as she was sure that the dean would take care of him, and even make it all right at Venice.

Delighted at getting rid of him in so honourable a manner, I ran to the inn, told him what I had done, gave him the letter, and promised not to abandon him in the case of the dean's not giving him a warm welcome. I got him a good carriage, and started him off the next day at daybreak. Four days after, Balbi wrote that the dean had received him with great kindness, that he had given him a room in the deanery, that he had dressed him as an abbe, that he had introduced him to the Prince-Bishop of Armstadt, and that he had received assurances of his safety from the civil magistrates. Furthermore, the dean had promised to keep him till he obtained his secularization from Rome, and with it freedom to return to Venice, for as soon as he ceased to be a monk the Tribunal would have no lien upon him. Father Balbi finished by asking me to send him a few sequins for pocket-money, as he was too much of a gentleman to ask the dean who, quoth the ungrateful fellow, "is not gentleman enough to offer to give me anything." I gave him no answer.

As I was now alone in peace and quietness, I thought seriously of regaining my health, for my sufferings had given me nervous spasms which might become dangerous. I put myself on diet, and in three weeks I was perfectly well. In the meanwhile Madame Riviere came from Dresden with her son and two daughters. She was going to Paris to marry the elder. The son had been diligent, and would have passed for a young man of culture. The elder daughter, who was going to marry an actor, was extremely beautiful, an accomplished dancer, and played on the clavichord like a professional, and was altogether most charming and graceful. This pleasant family was delighted to see me again, and I thought myself fortunate when Madame Riviere, anticipating my wishes, intimated to me that my company as far as Paris would give them great pleasure. I had nothing to say respecting the expenses of the journey. I had to accept their offer in its entirety.

My design was to settle in Paris, and I took this stroke of fortune as an omen of success in the only town where the blind goddess freely dispenses her favours to those who leave themselves to be guided by her, and know how to take advantage of her gifts. And, as the reader will see by and by, I was not mistaken; but all the gifts of fortune were of no avail, since I abused them all by my folly. Fifteen months under the Leads should have made me aware of my weak points, but in point of fact I needed a little longer stay to learn how to cure myself of my failings.

Madame Riviere wished to take me with her, but she could not put off her departure, and I required a week's delay to get money and letters from Venice. She promised to wait a week in Strassburg, and we agreed that if possible I would join her there. She left Munich on the 18th of December.

Two days afterwards I got from Venice the bill of exchange for which I was waiting. I made haste to pay my debts, and immediately afterwards I started for Augsburg, not so much for the sake of seeing Father Balbi, as because I wanted to make the acquaintance of the kindly dean who had rid me of him. I reached Augsburg in seven hours after leaving Munich, and I went immediately to the house of the good ecclesiastic. He was not in, but I found Balbi in an abbe's dress, with his hair covered with white powder, which set off in a new but not a pleasing manner the beauties of his complexion of about the same colour as a horse chestnut. Balbi was under forty, but he was decidedly ugly, having one of those faces in which baseness, cowardice, impudence, and malice are plainly expressed, joining to this advantage a tone of voice and manners admirably calculated to repulse anyone inclined to do him a service. I found him comfortably housed, well looked after, and well clad; he had books and all the requisites for writing. I complimented him upon his situation, calling him a fortunate fellow, and applying the same epithet to myself for having gained him all the advantages he enjoyed, and the hope of one day becoming a secular priest. But the ungrateful hound, instead of thanking me, reproached me for having craftily rid myself of him, and added that, as I was going to Paris, I might as well take him with me, as the dullness of Augsburg was almost killing him.

"What do you want at Paris?"

"What do you want yourself?"

"To put my talents to account."

"So do I."

"Well, then, you don't require me, and can fly on your own wings. The people who are taking me to Paris would probably not care for me if I had you for a companion."

"You promised not to abandon me."

"Can a man who leaves another well provided for and an assured future be said to abandon him?"

"Well provided! I have not got a penny."

"What do you want with money? You have a good table, a good lodging, clothes, linen, attendance, and so forth. And if you want pocket-money, why don't you ask your brethren the monks?"

"Ask monks for money? They take it, but they don't give it."

"Ask your friends, then."

"I have no friends."

"You are to be pitied, but the reason probably is that you have never been a friend to anyone. You ought to say masses, that is a good way of getting money."

"I am unknown."

"You must wait, then, till you are known, and then you can make up for lost time."

"Your suggestions are idle; you will surely give me a few sequins."

"I can't spare any."

"Wait for the dean. He will be back to-morrow. You can talk to him and persuade him to lend me some money. You can tell him that I will pay it back."

"I cannot wait, for I am setting out on my journey directly, and were he here this moment I should not have the face to tell him to lend you money after all his generous treatment of you, and when he or anyone can see that you have all you need."

After this sharp dialogue I left him, and travelling post I set out, displeased with myself for having given such advantages to a man wholly unworthy of them. In the March following I had a letter from the good Dean Bassi, in which he told me how Balbi had run away, taking with him one of his servant girls, a sum of money, a gold watch, and a dozen silver spoons and forks. He did not know where he was gone.

Towards the end of the same year I learnt at Paris that the wretched man had taken refuge at Coire, the capital of the Grisons, where he asked to be made a member of the Calvinistic Church, and to be recognized as lawful husband of the woman with him; but in a short time the community discovered that the new convert was no good, and expelled him from the bosom of the Church of Calvin. Our ne'er-do-well having no more money, his wife left him, and he, not knowing what to do next, took the desperate step of going to Bressa, a town within the Venetian territory, where he sought the governor, telling him his name, the story of his flight, and his repentance, begging the governor to take him under his protection and to obtain his pardon.

The first effect of the podesta's protection was that the penitent was imprisoned, and he then wrote to the Tribunal to know what to do with him. The Tribunal told him to send Father Balbi in chains to Venice, and on his arrival Messer-Grande gave him over to the Tribunal, which put him once more under the Leads. He did not find Count Asquin there, as the Tribunal, out of consideration for his great age, had moved him to The Fours a couple of months after our escape.

Five or six years later, I heard that the Tribunal, after keeping the unlucky monk for two years under the Leads, had sent him to his convent. There, his superior fearing lest his flock should take contagion from this scabby sheep, sent him to their original monastery near Feltre, a lonely building on a height. However, Balbi did not stop there six months. Having got the key of the fields, he went to Rome, and threw himself at the feet of Pope Rezzonico, who absolved him of his sins, and released him from his monastic vows. Balbi, now a secular priest, returned to Venice, where he lived a dissolute and wretched life. In 1783 he died the death of Diogenes, minus the wit of the cynic.

At Strassburg I rejoined Madame Riviere and her delightful family, from whom I received a sincere and hearty welcome. We were staying at the "Hotel de l'Esprit," and we passed a few days there most pleasurably, afterwards setting out in an excellent travelling carriage for Paris the Only, Paris the Universal. During the journey I thought myself bound to the expense of making it a pleasant one, as I had not to put my hand in my pocket for other expenses. The charms of Mdlle. Riviere enchanted me, but I should have esteemed myself wanting in gratitude and respect to this worthy family if I had darted at her a single amorous glance, or if I had let her suspect my feelings for her by a single word. In fact I thought myself obliged to play the heavy father, though my age did not fit me for the part, and I lavished on this agreeable family all the care which can be given in return for pleasant society, a seat in a comfortable travelling carriage, an excellent table, and a good bed.

We reached Paris on the 5th of January, 1757, and I went to the house of my friend Baletti, who received me with open arms, and assured me that though I had not written he had been expecting me, since he judged that I would strive to put the greatest possible distance between myself and Venice, and he could think of no other retreat for me than Paris. The whole house kept holiday when my arrival became known, and I have never met with more sincere regard than in that delightful family. I greeted with enthusiasm the father and mother, whom I found exactly the same as when I had seen them last in 1752, but I was struck with astonishment at the daughter whom I had left a child, for she was now a tall and well-shaped girl. Mdlle. Baletti was fifteen years old, and her mother had brought her up with care, had given her the best masters, virtue, grace, talents, a good manner, tact, a knowledge of society-in short, all that a clever mother can give to a dear daughter.

After finding a pleasant lodging near the Baletti's, I took a coach and went to the "Hotel de Bourbon" with the intention of calling on M. de Bernis, who was then chief secretary for foreign affairs. I had good reasons for relying on his assistance. He was out; he had gone to Versailles. At Paris one must go sharply to work, and, as it is vulgarly but forcibly said, "strike while the iron's hot." As I was impatient to see what kind of a reception I should get from the liberal-minded lover of my fair M—— M——, I went to the Pont-Royal, took a hackney coach, and went to Versailles. Again bad luck!

Our coaches crossed each other on the way, and my humble equipage had not caught his excellency's eye. M. de Bernis had returned to Paris with Count de Castillana, the ambassador from Naples, and I determined to return also; but when I got to the gate I saw a mob of people running here and there in the greatest confusion, and from all sides I heard the cry, "The king is assassinated! The king is assassinated!"

My frightened coachman only thought of getting on his way, but the coach was stopped. I was made to get out and taken to the guard-room, where there were several people already, and in less than three minutes there were twenty of us, all under arrest, all astonished at the situation, and all as much guilty as I was. We sat glum and silent, looking at each other without daring to speak. I knew not what to think, and not believing in enchantment I began to think I must be dreaming. Every face expressed surprise, as everyone, though innocent, was more or less afraid.

We were not left in this disagreeable position for long, as in five minutes an officer came in, and after some polite apologies told us we were free.

"The king is wounded," he said, "and he has been taken to his room. The assassin, whom nobody knows, is under arrest. M. de la Martiniere is being looked for everywhere."

As soon as I had got back to my coach, and was thinking myself lucky for being there, a gentlemanly-looking young man came up to me and besought me to give him a seat in my coach, and he would gladly pay half the fare; but in spite of the laws of politeness I refused his request. I may possibly have been wrong. On any other occasion I should have been most happy to give him a place, but there are times when prudence does not allow one to be polite. I was about three hours on the way, and in this short time I was overtaken every minute by at least two hundred couriers riding at a breakneck pace. Every minute brought a new courier, and every courier shouted his news to the winds. The first told me what I already knew; then I heard that the king had been bled, that the wound was not mortal, and finally, that the wound was trifling, and that his majesty could go to the Trianon if he liked.

Fortified with this good news, I went to Silvia's and found the family at table. I told them I had just come from Versailles.

"The king has been assassinated."

"Not at all; he is able to go to the Trianon, or the Parc-aux-cerfs, if he likes. M. de la Martiniere has bled him, and found him to be in no danger. The assassin has been arrested, and the wretched man will be burnt, drawn with red-hot pincers, and quartered."

This news was soon spread abroad by Silvia's servants, and a crowd of the neighbours came to hear what I had to say, and I had to repeat the same thing ten times over. At this period the Parisians fancied that they loved the king. They certainly acted the part of loyal subjects to admiration. At the present day they are more enlightened, and would only love the sovereign whose sole desire is the happiness of his people, and such a king—the first citizens of a great nation—not Paris and its suburbs, but all France, will be eager to love and obey. As for kings like Louis XV, they have become totally impracticable; but if there are any such, however much they may be supported by interested parties, in the eyes of public opinion they will be dishonoured and disgraced before their bodies are in a grave and their names are written in the book of history.

VII

The Minister of Foreign Affairs M. de Boulogne, the Comptroller—M. le Duc de Choiseul—M. Paris du Vernai—Establishment of the Lottery—My Brother's Arrival at Paris; His Reception by the Academy

Once more, then, I was in Paris, which I ought to regard as my fatherland, since I could return no more to that land which gave me birth: an unworthy country, yet, in spite of all, ever dear to me, possibly on account of early impressions and early prejudices, or possibly because the beauties of Venice are really unmatched in the world. But mighty Paris is a place of good luck or ill, as one takes it, and it was my part to catch the favouring gale.

Paris was not wholly new to me, as my readers know I had spent two years there, but I must confess that, having then no other aim than to pass the time pleasantly, I had merely devoted myself to pleasure and enjoyment. Fortune, to whom I had paid no court, had not opened to me her golden doors; but I now felt that I must treat her more reverently, and attach myself to the throng of her favoured sons whom she loads with her gifts. I understood now that the nearer one draws to the sun the more one feels the warmth of its rays. I saw that to attain my end I should have to employ all my mental and physical talents, that I must make friends of the great, and take cue from all whom I found it to be my interest to please. To follow the plans suggested by these thoughts, I saw that I must avoid what is called bad company, that I must give up my old habits and pretensions, which would be sure to make me enemies, who would have no scruple in representing me as a trifler, and not fit to be trusted with affairs of any importance.

I think I thought wisely, and the reader, I hope, will be of the same opinion. "I will be reserved," said I, "in what I say and what I do, and thus I shall get a reputation for discretion which will bring its reward."

I was in no anxiety on the score of present needs, as I could reckon on a monthly allowance of a hundred crowns, which my adopted father, the good and generous M. de Bragadin, sent me, and I found this sum sufficient in the meanwhile, for with a little self-restraint one can live cheaply at Paris, and cut a good figure at the same time. I was obliged to wear a good suit of clothes, and to have a decent lodging; for in all large towns the most important thing is outward show, by which at the beginning one is always judged. My anxiety was only for the pressing needs of the moment, for to speak the truth I had neither clothes nor linen—in a word, nothing.

If my relations with the French ambassador are recalled, it will be found natural that my first idea was to address myself to him, as I knew him sufficiently well to reckon on his serving me.

Being perfectly certain that the porter would tell me that my lord was engaged, I took care to have a letter, and in the morning I went to the Palais Bourbon. The porter took my letter, and I gave him my address and returned home.

Wherever I went I had to tell the story of my escape from The Leads. This became a service almost as tiring as the flight itself had been, as it took me two hours to tell my tale, without the slightest bit of fancy-work; but I had to be polite to the curious enquirers, and to pretend that I believed them moved by the most affectionate interest in my welfare. In general, the best way to please is to take the benevolence of all with whom one has relation for granted.

I supped at Silvia's, and as the evening was quieter than the night before, I had time to congratulate myself on all the friendship they shewed me. The girl was, as I had said, fifteen years old, and I was in every way charmed with her. I complimented the mother on the good results of her education, and I did not even think of guarding myself from falling a victim to her charms. I had taken so lately such well-founded and philosophical resolutions, and I was not yet sufficiently at my ease to value the pain of being tempted. I left at an early hour, impatient to see what kind of an answer the minister had sent me. I had not long to wait, and I received a short letter appointing a meeting for two o'clock in the afternoon. It may be guessed that I was punctual, and my reception by his excellence was most flattering. M. de Bernis expressed his pleasure at seeing me after my fortunate escape, and at being able to be of service to me. He told me that M—— M—— had informed him of my escape, and he had flattered himself that the first person I should go and see in Paris would be himself. He shewed me the letters from M—— M—— relating to my arrest and escape, but all the details in the latter were purely imaginary and had no foundation in fact. M—— M—— was not to blame, as she could only write what she had heard, and it was not easy for anyone besides myself to know the real circumstances of my escape. The charming nun said that, no longer buoyed up by the hope of seeing either of the men who alone had made her in love with life, her existence had become a burden to her, and she was unfortunate in not being able to take any comfort in religion. "C——C—— often comes to see me," she said, "but I grieve to say she is not happy with her husband."

I told M. de Bernis that the account of my flight from The Leads, as told by our friend, was wholly inaccurate, and I would therefore take the liberty of writing out the whole story with the minutest details. He challenged me to keep my word, assuring me that he would send a copy to M—— M——, and at the same time, with the utmost courtesy, he put a packet of a hundred Louis in my hand, telling me that he would think what he could do for me, and would advise me as soon as he had any communication to make.

Thus furnished with ample funds, my first care was for my dress; and this done I went to work, and in a week sent my generous protector the result, giving him permission to have as many copies printed as he liked, and to make any use he pleased of it to interest in my behalf such persons as might be of service to me.

Three weeks after, the minister summoned me to say that he had spoken of me to M. Erizzo, the Venetian ambassador, who had nothing to say against me, but for fear of embroiling himself with the State Inquisitors declined to receive me. Not wanting anything from him—his refusal did me no harm. M. de Bernis then told me that he had given a copy of my history to Madame la Marquise de Pompadour, and he promised to take the first opportunity of presenting me to this all-powerful lady. "You can present yourself, my dear Casanova," added his excellence, "to the Duc de Choiseul, and M. de Boulogne, the comptroller. You will be well received, and with a little wit you ought to be able to make good use of the letter. He himself will give you the cue, and you will see that he who listens obtains. Try to invent some useful plan for the royal exchequer; don't let it be complicated or chimerical, and if you don't write it out at too great length I will give you my opinion on it."

I left the minister in a pleased and grateful mood, but extremely puzzled to find a way of increasing the royal revenue. I knew nothing of finance, and after racking my brains all that I could think of was new methods of taxation; but all my plans were either absurd or certain to be unpopular, and I rejected them all on consideration.

As soon as I found out that M. de Choiseul was in Paris I called on him. He received me in his dressing-room, where he was writing while his valet did his hair. He stretched his politeness so far as to interrupt himself several times to ask me questions, but as soon as I began to reply his grace began to write again, and I suspect did not hear what I was saying; and though now and again he seemed to be looking at me, it was plain that his eyes and his thoughts were occupied on different objects. In spite of this way of receiving visitors—or me, at all events, M. de Choiseul was a man of wit.

When he had finished writing he said in Italian that M. de Bernis had told him of some circumstances of my escape, and he added,

"Tell me how you succeeded."

"My lord, it would be too long a story; it would take me at least two hours, and your grace seems busy."

"Tell me briefly about it."

"However much I speak to the point, I shall take two hours."

"You can keep the details for another time."

"The story is devoid of interest without the details."

"Well, well, you can tell me the whole story in brief, without losing much of the interest."

"Very good; after that I can say no more. I must tell your lordship, then, that, the State Inquisitors shut me up under the Leads; that after fifteen months and five days of imprisonment I succeeded in piercing the roof; that after many difficulties I reached the chancery by a window, and broke open the door; afterwards I got to St. Mark's Place, whence, taking a gondola which bore me to the mainland, I arrived at Paris, and have had the honour to pay my duty to your lordship."

"But. . . what are The Leads?"

"My lord, I should take a quarter of an hour, at least, to explain."

"How did you pierce the roof?"

"I could not tell your lordship in less than half an hour."

"Why were you shut up?"

"It would be a long tale, my lord."

"I think you are right. The interest of the story lies chiefly in the details."

"I took the liberty of saying as much to your grace."

"Well, I must go to Versailles, but I shall be delighted if you will come and see me sometimes. In the meanwhile, M. Casanova, think what I can do for you."

I had been almost offended at the way in which M. de Choiseul had received me, and I was inclined to resent it; but the end of our conversation, and above all the kindly tone of his last words, quieted me, and I left him, if not satisfied, at least without bitterness in my heart.

From him I went to M. de Boulogne's, and found him a man of quite a different stamp to the duke—in manners, dress, and appearance. He received me with great politeness, and began by complimenting me on the high place I enjoyed in the opinion of M. de Bernis, and on my skill in matters of finance.

I felt that no compliment had been so ill deserved, and I could hardly help bursting into laughter. My good angel, however, made me keep my countenance.

M. de Boulogne had an old man with him, every feature bore the imprint of genius, and who inspired me with respect.

"Give me your views;" said the comptroller, "either on paper or 'viva voce'. You will find me willing to learn and ready to grasp your ideas. Here is M. Paris du Vernai, who wants twenty millions for his military school; and he wishes to get this sum without a charge on the state or emptying the treasury."

"It is God alone, sir, who has the creative power."

"I am not a god," said M. du Vernai, "but for all that I have now and then created but the times have changed."

"Everything," I said, "is more difficult than it used to be; but in spite of difficulties I have a plan which would give the king the interest of a hundred millions."

"What expense would there be to the Crown?"

"Merely the cost of receiving."

"The nation, then, would furnish the sum in question?"

"Undoubtedly, but voluntarily."

"I know what you are thinking of."

"You astonish me, sir, as I have told nobody of my plan."

"If you have no other engagement, do me the honour of dining with me to-morrow, and I will tell you what your project is. It is a good one, but surrounded, I believe, with insuperable difficulties. Nevertheless, we will talk it over and see what can be done. Will you come?"

"I will do myself that honour."

"Very good, I will expect you at Plaisance."

After he had gone, M. de Boulogne praised his talents and honesty. He was the brother of M. de Montmartel, whom secret history makes the father of Madame de Pompadour, for he was the lover of Madame Poisson at the same time as M. le Normand.

I left the comptroller's and went to walk in the Tuileries, thinking over the strange stroke of luck which had happened to me. I had been told that twenty millions were wanted, and I had boasted of being able to get a hundred, without the slightest idea of how it was to be done; and on that a well-known man experienced in the public business had asked me to dinner to convince me that he knew what my scheme was. There was something odd and comic about the whole affair; but that corresponded very well with my modes of thought and action. "If he thinks he is going to pump me," said I, "he will find himself mistaken. When he tells me what the plan is, it will rest with me to say he has guessed it or he is wrong as the inspiration of the moment suggests. If the question lies within my comprehension I may, perhaps, be able to suggest something new; and if I understand nothing I will wrap myself up in a mysterious silence, which sometimes produces a good effect. At all events, I will not repulse Fortune when she appears to be favourable to me."

M. de Bernis had only told M. de Boulogne that I was a financier to get me a hearing, as otherwise he might have declined to see me. I was sorry not to be master, at least, of the jargon of the business, as in that way men have got out of a similar difficulty, and by knowing the technical terms, and nothing more, have made their mark. No matter, I was bound to the engagement. I must put a good face on a bad game, and if necessary pay with the currency of assurance. The next morning I took a carriage, and in a pensive mood I told the coachman to take me to M. du Vernai's, at Plaisance—a place a little beyond Vincennes.

I was set down at the door of the famous man who, forty years ago, had rescued France on the brink of the precipice down which Law had almost precipitated her. I went in and saw a great fire burning on the hearth, which was surrounded by seven or eight persons, to whom I was introduced as a friend of the minister for foreign affairs and of the comptroller; afterwards he introduced these gentlemen to me, giving to each his proper title, and I noted that four of them were treasury officials. After making my bow to each, I gave myself over to the worship of Harpocrates, and without too great an air of listening was all ears and eyes.

The conversation at first was of no special interest as they were talking of the Seine being frozen over, the ice being a foot thick. Then came the recent death of M. de Fontenelle, then the case of Damien, who would confess nothing, and of the five millions his trial would cost the Crown. Then coming to war they praised M. de Soubise, who had been chosen by the king to command the army. Hence the transition was easy to the expenses of the war, and how they were to be defrayed.

I listened and was weary, for all they said was so full of technicalities that I could not follow the meaning; and if silence can ever be imposing, my determined silence of an hour and a half's duration ought to have made me seem a very important personage in the eyes of these gentlemen. At last, just as I was beginning to yawn, dinner was announced, and I was another hour and a half without opening my mouth, except to do honour to an excellent repast. Directly the dessert had been served, M. du Vernai asked me to follow him into a neighbouring apartment, and to leave the other guests at the table. I followed him, and we crossed a hall where we found a man of good aspect, about fifty years old, who followed us into a closet and was introduced to me by M. du Vernai under the name of Calsabigi. Directly after, two superintendents of the treasury came in, and M. du Vernai smilingly gave me a folio book, saying,

"That, I think, M. Casanova, is your plan."

I took the book and read, Lottery consisting of ninety tickets, to be drawn every month, only one in eighteen to be a winning number. I gave him back the book and said, with the utmost calmness,

"I confess, sir, that is exactly my idea."

"You have been anticipated, then; the project is by M. de Calsabigi here."

"I am delighted, not at being anticipated, but to find that we think alike; but may I ask you why you have not carried out the plan?"

"Several very plausible reasons have been given against it, which have had no decisive answers."

"I can only conceive one reason against it," said I, coolly; "perhaps the king would not allow his subjects to gamble."

"Never mind that, the king will let his subjects gamble as much as they like: the question is, will they gamble?"

"I wonder how anyone can have any doubt on that score, as the winners are certain of being paid."

"Let us grant, then, that they will gamble: how is the money to be found?"

"How is the money to be found? The simplest thing in the world. All you want is a decree in council authorizing you to draw on the treasury.

All I want is for the nation to believe that the king can afford to pay a hundred millions."

"A hundred millions!"

"Yes, a hundred millions, sir. We must dazzle people."

"But if France is to believe that the Crown can afford to pay a hundred millions, it must believe that the Crown can afford to lose a hundred millions, and who is going to believe that? Do you?"

"To be sure I do, for the Crown, before it could lose a hundred millions, would have received at least a hundred and fifty millions, and so there need be no anxiety on that score."

"I am not the only person who has doubts on the subject. You must grant the possibility of the Crown losing an enormous sum at the first drawing?"

"Certainly, sir, but between possibility and reality is all the region of the infinite. Indeed, I may say that it would be a great piece of good fortune if the Crown were to lose largely on the first drawing."

"A piece of bad fortune, you mean, surely?"

"A bad fortune to be desired. You know that all the insurance companies are rich. I will undertake to prove before all the mathematicians in Europe that the king is bound to gain one in five in this lottery. That is the secret. You will confess that the reason ought to yield to a mathematical proof?"

"Yes, of course; but how is it that the Castelletto cannot guarantee the Crown a certain gain?"

"Neither the Castelletto nor anybody in the world can guarantee absolutely that the king shall always win. What guarantees us against any suspicion of sharp practice is the drawing once a month, as then the public is sure that the holder of the lottery may lose."

"Will you be good enough to express your sentiments on the subject before the council?"

"I will do so with much pleasure."

"You will answer all objections?"

"I think I can promise as much."

"Will you give me your plan?"

"Not before it is accepted, and I am guaranteed a reasonable profit."

"But your plan may possibly be the same as the one before us."

"I think not. I see M. de Calsabigi for the first time, and as he has not shewn me his scheme, and I have not communicated mine to him, it is improbable, not to say impossible, that we should agree in all respects.

Besides, in my plan I clearly shew how much profit the Crown ought to get per annum."

"It might, therefore, be formed by a company who would pay the Crown a fixed sum?"

"I think not."

"Why?"

"For this reason. The only thing which would make the lottery pay, would be an irresistible current of public opinion in its favour. I should not care to have anything to do with it in the service of a company, who, thinking to increase their profits, might extend their operations—a course which would entail certain loss."

"I don't see how."

"In a thousand ways which I will explain to you another time, and which I am sure you can guess for yourself. In short, if I am to have any voice in the matter, it must be a Government lottery or nothing."

"M. de Calsabigi thinks so, too."

"I am delighted to hear it, but not at all surprised; for, thinking on the same lines, we are bound to arrive at the same results."

"Have you anybody ready for the Castelletto?"

"I shall only want intelligent machines, of whom there are plenty in France."

I went out for a moment and found them in groups on my return, discussing my project with great earnestness.

M. Calsabigi after asking me a few questions took my hand, which he shook heartily, saying he should like to have some further conversation with me; and returning the friendly pressure, I told him that I should esteem it as an honour to be numbered amongst his friends. Thereupon I left my address with M. du Vernai and took my leave, satisfied, by my inspection of the faces before me, that they all had a high opinion of my talents.

Three days after, M. de Calsabigi called on me; and after receiving him in my best style I said that if I had not called on him it was only because I did not wish to be troublesome. He told me that my decisive way of speaking had made a great impression, and he was certain that if I cared to make interest with the comptroller we could set up the lottery and make a large profit.

"I think so, too," said I, "but the financiers will make a much larger profit, and yet they do not seem anxious about it. They have not communicated with me, but it is their look-out, as I shall not make it my chief aim."

"You will undoubtedly hear something about it today, for I know for a fact that M. de Boulogne has spoken of you to M. de Courteuil."

"Very good, but I assure you I did not ask him to do so."

After some further conversation he asked me, in the most friendly manner possible, to come and dine with him, and I accepted his invitation with a great pleasure; and just as we were starting I received a note from M. de Bernis, in which he said that if I could come to Versailles the next day he would present me to Madame de Pompadour, and that I should have an opportunity of seeing M. de Boulogne.

In high glee at this happy chance, less from vanity than policy I made M. de Calsabigi read the letter, and I was pleased to see him opening his eyes as he read it.

"You can force Du Vernai himself to accept the lottery," he said, "and your fortune is made if you are not too rich already to care about such matters."

"Nobody is ever rich enough to despise good fortune, especially when it is not due to favour."

"Very true. We have been doing our utmost for two years to get the plan accepted, and have met with nothing beyond foolish objections which you have crushed to pieces. Nevertheless, our plans must be very similar. Believe me it will be best for us to work in concert, for by yourself you would find insuperable difficulties in the working, and you will find no 'intelligent machines' in Paris. My brother will do all the work, and you will be able to reap the advantages at your ease."

"Are you, then, not the inventor of the scheme which has been shewn me?"

"No, it is the work of my brother."

"Shall I have the pleasure or seeing him?"

"Certainly. His body is feeble, but his mind is in all its vigour. We shall see him directly."

The brother was not a man of a very pleasing appearance, as he was covered with a kind of leprosy; but that did not prevent him having a good appetite, writing, and enjoying all his bodily and intellectual faculties; he talked well and amusingly. He never went into society, as, besides his personal disfigurement, he was tormented with an irresistible and frequent desire of scratching himself, now in one place, and now in another; and as all scratching is accounted an abominable thing in Paris, he preferred to be able to use his fingernails to the pleasures of society. He was pleased to say that, believing in God and His works, he was persuaded his nails had been given him to procure the only solace he was capable of in the kind of fury with which he was tormented.

"You are a believer, then, in final causes? I think you are right, but still I believe you would have scratched yourself if God had forgotten to give you any nails."

My remarks made him laugh, and he then began to speak of our common business, and I soon found him to be a man of intellect. He was the elder of the two brothers, and a bachelor. He was expert in all kinds of calculations, an accomplished financier, with a universal knowledge of commerce, a good historian, a wit, a poet, and a man of gallantry. His birthplace was Leghorn, he had been in a Government office at Naples, and had come to Paris with M. de l'Hopital. His brother was also a man of learning and talent, but in every respect his inferior.

He shewed me the pile of papers, on which he had worked out all the problems referring to the lottery.

"If you think you can do without me," said he, "I must compliment you on your abilities; but I think you will find yourself mistaken, for if you have no practical knowledge of the matter and no business men to help you, your theories will not carry you far. What will you do after you have obtained the decree? When you speak before the council, if you take my advice, you will fix a date after which you are not to be held responsible—that is to say, after which you will have nothing more to do with it. Unless you do so, you will be certain to encounter trifling and procrastination which will defer your plan to the Greek Kalends. On the other hand, I can assure you that M. du Vernai would be very glad to see us join hands:"

Very much inclined to take these gentlemen into partnership, for the good reason that I could not do without them, but taking care that they should suspect nothing, I went down with the younger brother, who introduced me to his wife before dinner. I found present an old lady well known at Paris under the name of General La Mothe, famous for her former beauty and her gout, another lady somewhat advanced in years, who was called Baroness Blanche, and was still the mistress of M. de Vaux, another styled the President's lady, and a fourth, fair as the dawn, Madame Razzetti, from Piedmont, the wife of one of the violin players at the opera, and said to be courted by M. de Fondpertuis, the superintendent of the opera.

We sat down to dinner, but I was silent and absorbed, all my thoughts being monopolized by the lottery. In the evening, at Silvia's,

I was pronounced absent and pensive, and so I was in spite of the sentiment with which Mademoiselle Baletti inspired me—a sentiment which every day grew in strength.

I set out for Versailles next morning two hours before day-break, and was welcomed by M. de Bernis, who said he would bet that but for him I should never have discovered my talent for finance.

"M. de Boulogne tells me you astonished M. du Vernai, who is generally esteemed one of the acutest men in France. If you will take my advice, Casanova, you will keep up that acquaintance and pay him assiduous court. I may tell you that the lottery is certain to be established, that it will be your doing, and that you ought to make something considerable out of it. As soon as the king goes out to hunt, be at hand in the private apartments, and I will seize a favourable moment for introducing you to the famous marquise. Afterwards go to the Office for Foreign Affairs, and introduce yourself in my name to the Abbe de la Ville. He is the chief official there, and will give you a good reception."

M. de Boulogne told me that, as soon as the council of the military school had given their consent, he would have the decree for the establishment of the lottery published, and he urged me to communicate to him any ideas which I might have on the subject of finance.

At noon Madame de Pompadour passed through the private apartments with the Prince de Soubise, and my patron hastened to point me out to the illustrious lady. She made me a graceful curtsy, and told me that she had been much interested in the subject of my flight.

"Do you go," said she, "to see your ambassador?"

"I shew my respect to him, madam, by keeping away."

"I hope you mean to settle in France."

"It would be my dearest wish to do so, madam, but I stand in need of patronage, and I know that in France patronage is only given to men of talent, which is for me a discouraging circumstance."

"On the contrary, I think you have reason to be hopeful, as you have some good friends. I myself shall be delighted if I can be of any assistance to you."

As the fair marquise moved on, I could only stammer forth my gratitude.

I next went to the Abbe de la Ville, who received me with the utmost courtesy, and told me that he would remember me at the earliest opportunity.

　　　　　　　　　　　　　　　　　　　GIACOMO CASANOVA

Versailles was a beautiful spot, but I had only compliments and not invitations to expect there, so after leaving M. de la Ville I went to an inn to get some dinner. As I was sitting down, an abbe of excellent appearance, just like dozens of other French abbes, accosted me politely, and asked me if I objected to our dining together. I always thought the company of a pleasant man a thing to be desired, so I granted his request; and as soon as he sat down he complimented me on the distinguished manner in which I had been treated by M. de la Ville. "I was there writing a letter," said he, "and I could hear all the obliging things the abbe said to you. May I ask, sir, how you obtained access to him?"

"If you really wish to know, I may be able to tell you."

"It is pure curiosity on my part."

"Well, then, I will say nothing, from pure prudence."

"I beg your pardon."

"Certainly, with pleasure."

Having thus shut the mouth of the curious impertinent, he confined his conversation to ordinary and more agreeable topics. After dinner, having no further business at Versailles, I made preparations for leaving, on which the abbe begged to be of my company. Although a man who frequents the society of abbes is not thought much more of than one who frequents the society of girls. I told him that as I was going to Paris in a public conveyance—far from its being a question of permission—I should be only too happy to have the pleasure of his company. On reaching Paris we parted, after promising to call on each other, and I went to Silvia's and took supper there. The agreeable mistress of the house complimented me on my noble acquaintances, and made me promise to cultivate their society.

As soon as I got back to my own lodging, I found a note from M. du Vernai, who requested me to come to the military school at eleven o'clock on the next day, and later in the evening Calsabigi came to me from his brother, with a large sheet of paper containing all the calculations pertaining to the lottery.

Fortune seemed to be in my favour, for this tabular statement came to me like a blessing from on high. Resolving, therefore, to follow the instructions which I pretended to receive indifferently. I went to the military school, and as soon as I arrived the conference began. M. d'Alembert had been requested to be present as an expert in arithmetical calculations. If M. du Vernai had been the only person to be consulted, this step would not have been necessary; but the council contained some obstinate heads who were unwilling to give in. The conference lasted three hours.

After my speech, which only lasted half an hour, M. de Courteuil summed up my arguments, and an hour was passed in stating objections which I refuted with the greatest ease. I finally told them that no man of honour and learning would volunteer to conduct the lottery on the understanding that it was to win every time, and that if anyone had the impudence to give such an undertaking they should turn him out of the room forthwith, for it was impossible that such an agreement could be maintained except by some roguery.

This had its effect, for nobody replied; and M. du Vernai remarked that if the worst came to the worst the lottery could be suppressed. At this I knew my business was done, and all present, after signing a document which M. du Vernai gave them, took their leave, and I myself left directly afterwards with a friendly leave-taking from M. du Vernal.

M. Calsabigi came to see me the next day, bringing the agreeable news that the affair was settled, and that all that was wanting was the publication of the decree.

"I am delighted to hear it," I said, "and I will go to M. de Boulogne's every day, and get you appointed chief administrator as soon as I know what I have got for myself."

I took care not to leave a stone unturned in this direction, as I knew that, with the great, promising and keeping a promise are two different things. The decree appeared a week after. Calsabigi was made superintendent, with an allowance of three thousand francs for every drawing, a yearly pension of four thousand francs for us both, and the chief of the lottery. His share was a much larger one than mine, but I was not jealous as I knew he had a greater claim than I. I sold five of the six offices that had been allotted to me for two thousand francs each, and opened the sixth with great style in the Rue St. Denis, putting my valet there as a clerk. He was a bright young Italian, who had been valet to the Prince de la Catolica, the ambassador from Naples.

The day for the first drawing was fixed, and notice was given that the winning numbers would be paid in a week from the time of drawing at the chief office.

With the idea of drawing custom to my office, I gave notice that all winning tickets bearing my signature would be paid at my office in twenty-four hours after the drawing. This drew crowds to my office and considerably increased my profits, as I had six per cent. on the receipts. A number of the clerks in the other offices were foolish enough to complain to Calsabigi that I had spoilt their gains, but he sent them about their business telling them that to get the better of me they had only to do as I did—if they had the money.

My first taking amounted to forty thousand francs. An hour after the drawing my clerk brought me the numbers, and shewed me that we had from seventeen to eighteen thousand francs to pay, for which I gave him the necessary funds.

Without my thinking of it I thus made the fortune of my clerk, for every winner gave him something, and all this I let him keep for himself.

The total receipts amounted to two millions, and the administration made a profit of six hundred thousand francs, of which Paris alone had contributed a hundred thousand francs. This was well enough for a first attempt.

On the day after the drawing I dined with Calsabigi at M. du Vernai's, and I had the pleasure of hearing him complain that he had made too much money. Paris had eighteen or twenty ternes, and although they were small they increased the reputation of the lottery, and it was easy to see that the receipts at the next drawing would be doubled. The mock assaults that were made upon me put me in a good humour, and Calsabigi said that my idea had insured me an income of a hundred thousand francs a year, though it would ruin the other receivers.

"I have played similar strokes myself," said M. du Vernai, "and have mostly succeeded; and as for the other receivers they are at perfect liberty to follow M. Casanova's example, and it all tends to increase the repute of an institution which we owe to him and to you."

At the second drawing a terne of forty thousand francs obliged me to borrow money. My receipts amounted to sixty thousand, but being obliged to deliver over my chest on the evening before the drawing, I had to pay out of my own funds, and was not repaid for a week.

In all the great houses I went to, and at the theatres, as soon as I was seen, everybody gave me money, asking me to lay it out as I liked and to send them the tickets, as, so far, the lottery was strange to most people. I thus got into the way of carrying about me tickets of all sorts, or rather of all prices, which I gave to people to choose from, going home in the evening with my pockets full of gold. This was an immense advantage to me, as kind of privilege which I enjoyed to the exclusion of the other receivers who were not in society, and did not drive a carriage like myself—no small point in one's favour, in a large town where men are judged by the state they keep. I found I was thus able to go into any society, and to get credit everywhere.

I had hardly been a month in Paris when my brother Francis, with whom I had parted in 1752, arrived from Dresden with Madame Sylvestre. He had been at Dresden for four years, taken up with the pursuit of his art, having copied all the battle pieces in the Elector's Galley. We were both of us glad to meet once more, but on my offering to see what my great friends could do for him with the Academicians, he replied with all an artist's pride that he was much obliged to me, but would rather not have any other patrons than his talents. "The French," said he, "have rejected me once, and I am far from bearing them ill-will on that account, for I would reject myself now if I were what I was then; but with their love of genius I reckon on a better reception this time."

His confidence pleased me, and I complimented him upon it, for I have always been of the opinion that true merit begins by doing justice to itself.

Francis painted a fine picture, which on being exhibited at the Louvre, was received with applause. The Academy bought the picture for twelve thousand francs, my brother became famous, and in twenty-six years he made almost a million of money; but in spite of that, foolish expenditure, his luxurious style of living, and two bad marriages, were the ruin of him.

A Note About the Author

Giacomo Casanova (1725–1798) was an Italian adventurer and author. Born in Venice, Casanova was the eldest of six siblings born to Gaetano Casanova and Zanetta Farussi, an actor and actress. Raised in a city noted for its cosmopolitanism, night life, and glamor, Casanova overcame a sickly childhood to excel in school, entering the University of Padua at the age of 12. After graduating in 1742 with a degree in law, he struggled to balance his work as a lawyer and low-level cleric with a growing gambling addiction. As scandals and a prison sentence threatened to derail his career in the church, Casanova managed to find work as a scribe for a powerful Cardinal in Rome, but was soon dismissed and entered military service for the Republic of Venice. Over the next several years, he left the service, succeeded as a professional gambler, and embarked on a Grand Tour of Europe. Towards the end of his life, Casanova worked on his exhaustive, scandalous memoirs, a 12-volume autobiography reflecting on a legendary life of romance and debauchery that brought him from the heights of aristocratic society to the lows of illness and imprisonment. Recognized for his self-styled sensationalism as much as he is for his detailed chronicling of 18th century European culture, Casanova is a man whose name is now synonymous with the kind of life he led—fast, fearless, and free.

A Note from the Publisher

Spanning many genres, from non-fiction essays to literature classics to children's books and lyric poetry, Mint Edition books showcase the master works of our time in a modern new package. The text is freshly typeset, is clean and easy to read, and features a new note about the author in each volume. Many books also include exclusive new introductory material. Every book boasts a striking new cover, which makes it as appropriate for collecting as it is for gift giving. Mint Edition books are only printed when a reader orders them, so natural resources are not wasted. We're proud that our books are never manufactured in excess and exist only in the exact quantity they need to be read and enjoyed.

bookfinity™

Discover more of your favorite classics with Bookfinity™.

- Track your reading with custom book lists.
- Get great book recommendations for your personalized Reader Type.
- Add reviews for your favorite books.
- AND MUCH MORE!

Visit **bookfinity.com** and take the fun Reader Type quiz to get started.

Enjoy our classic and modern companion pairings!

Classic & Modern

www.ingramcontent.com/pod-product-compliance
Lightning Source LLC
Chambersburg PA
CBHW021130020426
42331CB00005B/703